I SEE BY YOUR OUTFIT

Historic cowboy gear
of the Northern Plains

I SEE BY YOUR OUTFIT

HISTORIC COWBOY GEAR OF THE NORTHERN PLAINS

ILLUSTRATED WITH HISTORIC PHOTOGRAPHS

TOM LINDMIER & STEVE MOUNT

WITH A FOREWORD BY
JOHN P. LANGELLIER, PH.D.

HIGH PLAINS PRESS
GLENDO, WYOMING

10   9   8   7   6   5   4   3

The identification of individuals in historic photographs is sometimes difficult. If readers have additional information on the names of cowboys pictured in this book, please contact the authors at:

HIGH PLAINS PRESS
P.O. BOX 123LM
GLENDO, WYOMING 82213

Library of Congress Cataloging-in-Publication Data

Lindmier, Thomas A.
I see by your outfit
historic cowboy gear of the northern plains
Thomas A. Lindmier & Steven R. Mount :
with a foreword by John P. Langellier.
p. cm.
Includes bibliographical references and index.
ISBN 0-931271-34-7 (cloth : alk. paper).
ISBN 0-931271-33-9 (soft : alk. paper)
1. Cowboys--Wyoming--History.
2. Cowboys--Costume--Wyoming.
3. Wyoming--Social life and customs.
I. Mount, Steven R.
F761.L64 1995   95-39003
391'.04636'0978709034--dc20   CIP

The authors would like to especially acknowledge and thank the following:
—— Dr. Joseph Palen, Cheyenne, for his patience, knowledge and guidance in assuring the historical accuracy of this material;
—— Cynde Georgen for her expertise in proofreading and editing;
—— Paula Chavoya and her staff at the Wyoming State Museum Photograph Section for all their assistance and time expended in helping us search for appropriate historic photographs;
—— The staffs of these Wyoming museums:
   Wyoming Pioneer Memorial Museum, Douglas,
   American Heritage Center, Laramie,
   Anna Miller Museum, Newcastle,
   Fremont County Pioneer Museum, Lander,
   Sweetwater County Historical Society, Green River,
for their eagerness to open their historic photograph and museum collections for our research;
—— The late Tom Tisdale for sharing his knowledge and photographs;
—— Janette Chambers and Sally Ann Neiman for photographs from their family collections;
—— Jonita Sommers for research into the identifications and location of the "White Horse Roundup";
—— The Wyoming State Historical Society for the Lola Homsher Grant which provided the financial assistance we needed to acquire the historic photographs;
—— Our wives, Linda and Connie, for their patience and understanding.

C O N T E N T S

"The year 1994 marks the five-hundredth anniversary of the arrival of the first cattle in the Western Hemisphere." This opening sentence to David Dary's fine book, *Cowboy Culture: A Saga of Five Centuries,* could have gone on to say that the arrival of cattle also ultimately ushered in the creation of one of the New World's most enduring and colorful characters—the cowboy.

For generations the work, and the worker who performed it, were looked upon as menial. There was nothing particularly glamorous about dealing with cows—the herding, branding, calving and all the other difficult chores which occupied the vaquero, as he came to be known in Spanish.

Despite this, a certain esprit developed among this breed of men. In addition, right after the end of the American Civil War public recognition began to grow, especially as the drovers pushed their herds from Texas to the Kansas railheads in response to the clamor for beef to feed a growing nation. Even as the cowboy's image began to become more widely known after the 1860s, the buckaroos themselves started to capture some of the spirit of their world and to share it, privately at first, with their saddle

"pardners" in tall tales, song, and poetry. Sitting around campfires, in bunkhouses when there was no pay or time to go into a nearby community, or in saloons and other gathering places, cowboys practiced these folk arts for fellow cowboys. In the early days, they often borrowed from other traditions, particularly sea chanteys and sailor poetry.

Even as the cowpokes were celebrating their lifestyle among themselves, the transformation of the ordinary working cowpuncher into a larger-than-life romantic hero began to spread to a wider audience. In the last decades of the 1800s, dime novels and Wild West shows caught the imagination of a national and international audience. With the advent of films, this tradition of glorifying and exaggerating the cowboy was continued on in motion pictures featuring such pioneers of the silver screen as "Bronco Billy" Anderson, William S. Hart, Tom Mix and a legion of others who saddled up to ride the cinema trail.

Most of the stories depicted in movie theaters and later on television bore only a faint resemblance to the reality of cowboy life. So, too, did the appearance of the cowpunchers in these horse operas deviate from

← These unidentified cowboys are shown branding a calf near Douglas, Wyoming. The cowboy holding the calf's hind leg is wearing bib-overalls and moccasins, an unusual combination. *[Wyoming Pioneer Memorial Museum]*

what actually was worn on the trail and ranches. Few individuals have addressed this dichotomy in a serious way. Of course, William Foster Harris' 1955 *The Look of the Old West* provided a cursory look at the topic while Don Rickey's *$10 Horse $40 Saddle: Cowboy Clothing, Arms, Tools, and Horse Gear of the 1880s* expanded on the theme, as did Dary's *Cowboy Culture….* Yet, no systematic study of the subject has been published to date.

Tom Lindmier and Steve Mount, two natives of Wyoming, decided to take on this ambitious subject at least for their state, and have spent countless hours in public and private collections reviewing photographs, artifacts, and other sources to produce what may well be the prototype for further treatments of this topic on a state-by-state or even a regional basis. The years of diligent research by the two authors resulted in a well-documented and profusely illustrated book. For these reasons, this publication is a must for those interested in the cowboy as he appeared on the northern Great Plains in the last decades of the Victorian era and into the opening of the twentieth century.

JOHN P. LANGELLIER, PH D.
DIRECTOR OF PUBLICATIONS & PRODUCTIONS
GENE AUTRY WESTERN HERITAGE MUSEUM

It is not the intent of this book to delve into the romance of the cowboy or the evolution of the cattle industry. Our purpose is to illustrate and discuss cowboy clothing, implements, and horse equipment as they developed in Wyoming from 1870 until 1928. We will show how the cowboy actually appeared while working the range, not as he has been presented in modern books and movies.

In this volume we will, by use of historic photographs, original catalog illustrations, and photographs of existing museum pieces, elucidate the dress and equipment of the Wyoming cowboy. Primary source materials are used to produce the narrative for each individual item. These research sources include diaries and reminiscences, plus nineteenth- and twentieth-century catalogs from which the Wyoming cowboy and his suppliers purchased their wares and equipment.

Movie costumers, writers and illustrators have continually misrepresented the appearance of the nineteenth- and early twentieth-century cowboy with flippant disregard. Audiences have grown up with misconceptions about his style of clothing, horse equipment and weapons. Recently, however, a renewed interest in authenticity has revived attempts by Hollywood studios to provide accurate clothing and horse equipment for their actors. It is hoped that this work will assist the researcher in knowing what was worn and used by the Wyoming cowboy during the latter half of the nineteenth century and the first two decades of the twentieth century. When applicable, we have provided the dates when items were introduced or when they ceased to be available or popular.

In studying hundreds of historic photographs we have learned not to totally trust studio photographs as representing the true image of the Wyoming cowboy. The historic photographs of cowboys at work are perhaps more valuable than the studio photographs: while studio photographs often provide greater detail, they also show the cowboy out of his natural habitat, the open range. Just as today's cowboy posing for a photograph wears his new Stetson hat and his best clothes rather than his baseball cap and work clothes, the same was true for the historic cowboy.

We have also learned to scrutinize everything written in first-hand accounts. Although they are an invaluable resource, many were written twenty to fifty years later. Quite often facts became confused as the mind searched for details. For example, a cowboy might recall that he carried a .30−.30 Winchester in the 1880s when in fact this caliber rifle was not introduced until after 1895.

While our research centered in Wyoming, it should aid those interested in the true image of the cowboy throughout the entire Northern Plains area. Cowboys of the Southern Plains and the California-Oregon region are also explored to a limited degree because to gain a full understanding of the dress and gear of the Wyoming cowboy, we found we had to compare, contrast and examine cowboys of other areas as well.

The intertwining of ideas and methods from cowboys across the country, and even across national borders ultimately, produced what we know as the Wyoming cowboy.

← Some historic photographs raise as many questions as they answer. Here Elton Perry, 1902 Cheyenne Frontier Days Champion Bronco Buster, had his photo taken with his championship saddle and a most unlikely hat. Many working cowboys would have laughed Perry off the range if he'd appeared in this attire. One has to wonder if he posed in the hat as a joke or if the hat was actually a piece of apparel that he commonly wore. *[Joseph Palen collection]*

THE COWBOY'S LAMENT*

As I walked out in the streets of Laredo,
As I walked out in Laredo one day,
I spied a poor cowboy wrapped up in white linen,
Wrapped up in white linen as cold as the clay.

"I see by your outfit that you are a cowboy,"
These words he did say as I boldly stepped by,
"Come, sit down beside me and hear my sad story;
I was shot in the breast and I know I must die.

"It was once in the saddle I used to go dashing,
It was once in the saddle I used to be gay;
First to the dram-house, then to the card-house;
Got shot in the breast, I am dying today."

We beat the drum slowly and played the fife lowly,
And bitterly wept as we bore him along;
For we all loved our comrade, so brave, young, and handsome;
We all loved our comrade, although he done wrong.

_____

*These are four verses of the old cowboy song which has many variations
and many, many verses.

CHAPTER ONE

THE NORTHERN PLAINS COWBOY

← The cowboys all mounted white horses for this roundup photo taken at the upper spring near Bench Corrals in Meadow Canyon in 1897 near Big Piney, Wyoming. *Front row:* Archie Roberts, Ralph Friend, Al Davison, Al Osterhout, Ballie Johnson, Fred Schebell, James Mickelson, Amos W. Smith (foreman), Joe Anderson Hughes, Charles P. Budd, Ezra Swan, Grant Swan, and Jim Sykes *Back row:* Norris W. Griggs, Frank D. Ball, Doggie Edwards, George Richards (cook), Oscar Redick, and Fred Dubois (horse wrangler). *[American Heritage Center, University of Wyoming]*

The cowboy of the Northern American Plains has caught the imagination of the world more than any other figure in the opening of the frontier. Americans have long viewed the cowboy in a romantic light: dime novels, magazine stories and Buffalo Bill's Wild West Show glorified the cowboy as early as the 1870s. They presented the cowboy as a dashing figure glowing with good will and a tender heart, his superhuman courage making him capable of great deeds of valor. With time these wild and exciting feats ballooned until the nation and, indeed, the world, viewed the life of a cowboy as more exciting than it truly was or could have been. Owen Wister, Frederic Remington, Charles Russell, Will Rogers and others provided raw material for this legendary macho hero, some factual and some not.

And so the romance grew. The cowboy has been pictured as either a knightly figure above reproach or as a wild semi-outlaw, as undomesticated as the prairie he roamed. The truth presents a different image.

⌠ Addison Spaugh was general foreman of the Converse Cattle Company when it was located on Old Woman Creek near Lusk, Wyoming. This photograph was taken during the 1884 Roundup Number 15 on the Cheyenne River drainage. Spaugh's saddle was made by J.S. Collins. *[Wyoming State Museum]*

It must be remembered that the cowboy worked in a rural, unpopulated expanse of plains, allowing him little time to frequent the often riotous cow towns. Consequently, most of these young men had little opportunity to play the role of either villain or hero. Of course, there were outlaws among their numbers as within all classes of men. But most of these men were not nearly as "bad" as they have been represented. Nor was the common range cowhand always at the ready to rescue a woman in distress or "shoot it out" over a game of cards. Like most young men who have been isolated from civilization for months, however, when the cowboy visited a community he often indulged in excess, thus adding to his image of being wild and frivolous.

Of this man and his trade much has been recorded. Yet few people who are familiar with this type of life are willing to agree that any book on this subject is entirely correct. Perhaps this is due to the fact that the open range cattle industry, as a whole, suddenly appeared and disappeared within a single generation (except in a few isolated areas). Consequently, ranching on the unfenced northern range never had a chance to become fully standardized. Another reason

→ Jack Blackwell was roundup foreman for the 1884 Roundup Number 15. This photograph was taken that year. Note that his revolver is arranged for a "cross draw." *[Wyoming State Museum]*

for disagreement is that different regions of the plains had dissimilar conditions which affected ranching's development; the Texas cowboy, for example, encountered difficulties unlike those of his contemporaries from Wyoming, Colorado or Montana. Yet there were many elements common to both. Through the intermingling of cowboys from region to region, they shared their experiences and frequently utilized nearly the same techniques and equipment to accomplish their tasks.

The work of the cowboy was composed of never-ending variety, yet at times was totally monotonous. His lot included driving cattle herds, conducting roundups, branding calves, riding line, breaking horses, defending against thieves, building corrals and living quarters, and selecting beef cattle for market. He had to maintain his equipment and clothing, prepare meals, supply firewood and perform many other everyday tasks necessary to exist. During the winter he checked the herds, hunted predators and generally tried to survive the long season. Often cowboys were laid off for the winter and "rode the grub-line." By living alone for long periods and having to make ends meet, the cowboy developed

⌐ Sid Brace was an OW cowboy working on roundup 15 with Spaugh and Blackwell when this photograph was taken in 1884. *[American Heritage Center]*

resourcefulness and the ability to take care of himself in nearly any circumstance.

On the open ranges of Wyoming, the majority of the work was done during the spring and fall roundups. The work was hard, often involving a huge territory. During large roundups the cowboy could be out on the range for several months. The cattle of many ranches were gathered from the various ranges and separated according to brand. During the spring roundup, the calves were cut out and branded. During the fall roundup, the market cows were separated from the herd for shipment. These large roundups sometimes involved hundreds of men, many chuck wagons and usually a minimum of two horses per rider. As an example, Wyoming Roundup Number 15, in 1884, worked the Cheyenne River drainage. It took six weeks for nearly 290 men representing twenty-one ranches to work 400,000 head of cattle.

During the early 1870s, most of the cattle that stocked the Wyoming rangelands arrived from Texas. By 1873, however, cattle were being introduced into Wyoming from Colorado, Oregon, Nevada and Washington. As early as 1873, Herefords from

The headquarters of the Converse Cattle Company building near Lusk, Wyoming, 1884. A.A. Spaugh is standing in right doorway, C.E. "Dougie" Robinson is seated with book to Spaugh's left. A man named Williams is sitting left of Robinson. Bill Bail has the banjo. Jack Blackwell is holding the violin and sitting left of Bail. Alex Jordan is standing in second doorway in white shirt. George Ray is left of Jordan in dark shirt. Sid Brace is leaning on the building left of Ray.

The two men boxing are Frank Decastro (right) and Orville Vincent. Bill Mitchell, ranchman, is mounted on the horse nearest the house. F.A. Watt is mounted on the middle horse. Jim Cuttingham is second from left in background. Jesse Bailand is left of Cuttingham. George Umpheres is standing behind Joe Ryan who is leaning on the fence, and Frank D. Russell is standing at the horse's head in foreground. Others are unidentified. *[Wyoming State Museum]*

↙ Branding crew for the Converse Cattle Company (OW ranch) in 1884 in the Cheyenne River drainage. *[Wyoming Pioneer Memorial Museum, Douglas, Wyoming]*

↑ These cowboy, with bedrolls ready, were photographed at a roundup near Lusk, Wyoming, around the turn of the century. They rode near the 77 Ranch on Lance Creek with foreman Addison Spaugh. The riders are Bob Hester, Guy Shipley, Louis Ryan, Burr Shipley, Roy Rogers, Henry Bennett, Newt Dupes, and Charles Bright. *[Wyoming Pioneer Memorial Museum]*

Colorado were being sold in eastern markets. The Swan brothers began to raise and breed Herefords shortly thereafter.[1] The *Cheyenne* (Wyoming) *Daily Leader* states that during the summer of 1878, between 225,000 and 300,000 cattle were driven from Texas to the northern territories and that 100,000 head of cattle were trailed from Oregon and Washington Territories to beef markets in the east. Some of these were held on the ranges of Wyoming.

In 1878, Wyoming Territory assessment records showed an estimate of 375,000 cattle on the range.[2] The northwestern movement of cattle increased after the Indian Wars of 1876 and 1877. These Oregon and Washington cattle were of Durham, Hereford, Polled and Shorthorn stock and had many advantages over both Texas longhorns and cattle from the midwest. The midwestern cattle developed lung fever or pneumonia which killed many and reduced the strength and resistance of those that survived on the open range, while ticks were the bane of the longhorn. John K. Rollinson noted that:

> . . . the Texas longhorns, though admirably adapted to the open-range conditions, were not desirable cattle for the feeder. Their length of horn was a bar to close quartering in feed lots and to loading in cattle cars for shipment. Along with these objections, there was the ever-present tick, which became known on the range as the "Texas fever tick." It did but minimum of damage to the longhorn, for he was immune after many generations of tick fever in his blood, but the same tick was very hard on animals from other parts of the country where the tick was unknown.[3]

Livestock from the Pacific northwest were mostly of Durham blood, but not pure Durham reds or roans. They lacked color uniformity but they had fewer off colors than the Texas longhorn herds of duns, creams, brindles, bronco-faces and buckskins.[4] They tended to make heavier beef and brought better prices at market. When crossbred with the longhorn, a sturdy animal developed.

Regardless of the breed of cattle he was handling, the cowboy's work was hard. The food provided by the roundup chuck wagon cooks, however, made it worthwhile. Cooks competed with each other to prepare their best dishes, all for the honor of the "brand." At the end of a hard day the men from the various outfits came together for stories, news and good-natured joking. Practical jokes were a major

⌐ These two unidentified cowboys have roped an elk in the Lander, Wyoming area during the mid-1880s. The man on horseback has tapaderos on his stirrups. *[Fremont County Pioneer Museum]*

form of entertainment at these gatherings and woe to the cowboy who did not show a sense of humor when he was the brunt of a gag.

Riding a line was the main duty of the cowboy between roundups. This entailed living in isolated cabins, or line camps, located on the boundaries of the ranch's rangeland. The work consisted mainly of keeping the cattle from drifting off the rangelands. After the mid-1880s, barbed wire fencing began to be utilized for this purpose and the line rider primarily maintained the fence.

During the winter months the work on a ranch decreased. With this reduction in work, many cowboys were left unemployed. Some found temporary winter jobs and others rode the grub line. This particular type of line rider drifted from ranch to ranch, line camp to line camp, all winter long, living off the generosity of the cattlemen and cowboys. It was part of the range code never to turn away a hungry traveler, and this generally produced a prolonged visit. To the lonely cowboy in a line camp these visits were usually most welcome.

Historically, the supreme era of the American cowboy began with the end of the American Civil War. This was the romantic period of the open range, complete with epic cattle drives from Texas to the northern territories and states. These were the days of cattle empires, bloody range wars, and wide open cowtowns like Abilene, Dodge City and Cheyenne.

The romance ended tragically in the mid-1880s due to bad management, the collapse of the beef market and, especially, the unpredictable behavior of Mother Nature. Even with the poor management of absentee landowners and the collapse of the always-volatile beef market, the glory days of the cowboy might have continued had it not been for the disastrous winter of 1886–1887. This winter, with its ice storms, shrieking blizzards and mammoth snow drifts, decimated the large cattle herds and forced many of the cattle empires into ruin. After the snow

← Branding on the open range during the 1880s in Wyoming. The cattle are longhorns. *[Wyoming State Museum]*

melted and the winds died down, the northern plains cattle industry was altered forever and a more subdued type of ranching emerged, one involving fewer cattle, smaller ranges, and a renewed respect for the uncertainty of life.

Although it had changed dramatically, the open range cowboy's life drama did not end in 1886. This took another catalyst: the arrival of homesteaders and the barbed wire fence which slowly closed the open range.

The cattle industry survived and the cowboy continued to ply his trade, but the old free and expansive life had ended. Some cowboys were still needed to manage the fenced herds, but many suddenly found nothing but continual unemployment. Most of these unemployed cowboys found work in unrelated occupations, some established their own ranches, and a few turned to rustling.

In Wyoming prior to 1878, only the southern third of the state was open for settlement. The northern two-thirds, the western half of the Dakotas and Nebraska, and the southern half of Montana, were Indian territories. Thus the country south of the North Platte River was more or less crowded with ranches while the land north of the river was not. After 1878 however, following the final battles of the Indian Wars, Wyoming's northern ranges began to be settled by ranchers and others.

Toward the end of the nineteenth century and as the cattle industry entered the twentieth century, many of the old ways of managing stock began to disappear. The cowboy who wished to keep working was forced to learn the new skills associated with a more modern ranching industry, such as cutting and baling hay, vaccinating stock, building fence and farming. Although fewer cowboys were needed on a ranch, those that continued found their jobs generally more steady and permanent.

As with most things, progress forever altered the cowboy lifestyle. The automobile was probably the most significant factor in the twentieth century to change the livestock industry. Horses, once the only means of transportation, were replaced for many tasks by tractors and trucks. Not only did this cut down on the need for horses, it economized the rancher's time and reduced his need for ranch-hands. By the late 1930s and early 1940s, almost all vestiges of the early cowboy had disappeared, marking an inglorious end to the cowboy way of life. Gone like the roving herds of buffalo and the nomadic Indian, the range-drifting cowboy remained only in literature, art and photographs—and in the minds of people attempting to, in some way, relive this bygone era of American history.

Although they may have started with good intentions, western novelists and the film industry created a mythical cowboy that only in partial truth existed. Hollywood put hundreds of unemployed cowhands to work during the early part of the twentieth century as the public became enthralled with the romance of the wild west. Early silent films utilized these authentic cowboys as actors and extras, thus reflecting the cowboy's true image. But as "B" westerns became popular, authenticity was lost to romance as western heroes became knights in shining armor, wearing clothing with flash and sparkle to accent their pure and honest deeds. Saddles and gun leather were smothered with silver inlay and fancy designs, thus masking their utilitarian origins and purpose.

>⋅⋅⊶⋅○⋅⊷⋅⋅<

Who the cowboys of the Northern Plains were has been documented in numerous volumes. What has been ignored, for the most part, has been how they dressed and what kind of equipment they used and why. Like today's working cowboy, these men used purely functional clothing and equipment. Since the true nineteenth-century cowboy was disdainful of laborers, soldiers, townsmen and especially farmers, he prided himself in standing apart in his choice of clothing. He was generally not fancy in his dress and was very cautious of the shadow watcher or mail order cowboy who tried to imitate him. The true mark of the cowboy was his endurance, horsemanship, and skill with rope, gun and branding iron, not how he looked in his Stetson and Levi's.

A cowboy's horse equipment was functional (yet at times quite ornamental) and always of the best quality and craftsmanship he could afford.

It took an unusual breed of man to endure so many hardships yet still love the work. His clothing and equipment reflected the austere conditions in which the cowboy lived, yet history also shows that the working cowboy took a special pride in "his outfit."

↙ Cowboys in front of the E.K. Ranch at Kaycee, Wyoming in the 1890s. Note the calf in the foreground. The E.K. Ranch was one of several that belonged to the Frontier Land and Cattle Company. *[Wyoming State Museum]*

← The cowboys of the Pratt & Ferris Ranch near Lusk during the 1898 fall roundup. The photograph shows cowboys wearing a large variety of hats along with various styles of coats and sweaters. *[Wyoming State Museum]*

CLOTHING
COWBOY

The clothing selected by Wyoming's early cowboys, like that of people everywhere, depended upon prevailing styles, availability of fabrics or ready-to-wear items, weather, and cash on hand. Although it is easy to think of the early cattle era as one period, in reality what a cowboy wore in 1870 was not the same as what he wore in 1900. One of the most accurate descriptions comes from O. C. Lapp, a Black Hills cowboy who began his career at the age of 16, in 1887:

> ...about the price of a cow waddy's outfit those days—saddle, bridle, chaps, spurs, hat and breeches. Don't think there was a $60 saddle on the roundup in that neck of the woods. Those kinds of saddles and ten gallon hats came into vogue when the "Drug store and rodeo" cowboys became popular. A cowboy's outfit must have dropped in price to beat the band, for when I was ridin' you could buy a crackin' good pair of high heel boots at from $4 to $6; but I did buy a pair from Lon Ayers that he had made, but

← This studio portrait taken in 1904 of Sweetwater County Wyoming cowboys shows bound brims on three of the hats and a variety of suitcoats and ties. Shown seated are Noyes Chittim and Dode Welch. Standing are Grey Burnett and Eugene Jones. *[Fremont County (Wyoming) Pioneer Museum]*

they were too small for him, for $10. That old shoemaker down on Lame Johnny creek made them for Lon at a cost of $11...

Our California breeches cost us $7.50 a shot, while our Stetson hats could be bought either from Felix Poznansky or the L. Morris Co. for $5. And they were not the ten gallon variety, either as the aforesaid drug store and dude ranch would-be cowpunchers today [1956] wear.

Edward C. "Teddy Blue" Abbott was a cowboy from Nebraska who trailed cattle north from Texas in 1871, 1879 and 1883, and also worked cows in Wyoming. He knew first hand what clothing was worn during his lifetime. When recounting his past life, Abbott reflected in 1939 on the differences in clothing throughout the years he was a cowboy:

Most all of them were Southerners, and they were a wild reckless bunch. For dress they wore wide-brimmed beaver hats, black or brown with a low crown, fancy shirts, high heeled boots and sometimes a vest. Their clothes and saddles were all homemade. Most of them had an army coat with cape which was slicker and blanket too. ...As the business grew, great changes took place in their style of dress, but their boots and cigarettes have lasted nearly the same for more than sixty years. In place of the low-crowned hat of the seventies we had a high-crowned white Stetson hat, fancy shirts with pockets and striped or checked California pants made in Oregon City, the best pants ever made to ride in. In winter we had nice cloth overcoats with beaver collars and cuffs. [2]

Many of the early Wyoming cowboys originally came from rural Texas, accompanying herds north from this southern state. These origins had a direct impact on the type of clothing worn when they arrived in Wyoming. One of those cowboys was W. M. Shannon of Lytle, Texas. Shannon traveled northward in 1878 as a cowboy and described his clothing as "...made by hand. My mother and sisters spun and wove the cloth for our clothing." [3] Abbott stated that in 1879 he bought his first set of clothes: "...those were the first store clothes I had ever bought myself. Before that my mother made my clothes or they were bought for me...." [4]

While it is certain that not all of the cowboys trailing cattle from Texas wore home-spun clothing, it is fairly certain that many of those early cowboys at least possessed some garments of this nature.

A direct contrast can be seen in the clothing purchased by John Rollinson around 1900:

I bought a new Stetson hat of the proper shape and style for a cowman, also more woolen blankets and a sugan or two. I yet had some of the blue army shirts and wool army pants. I bought some heavy wool underwear and wool socks. [5]

Montgomery Ward established his mail order business in 1872, one of the first catalog businesses in the United States. Ward created a unique way for rural America to purchase needed clothing without making long trips to a community. General merchandise stores located within the various communities were another source for procuring clothing. In 1892, Floyd Bard bought his clothes in Buffalo, Wyoming, from a local business. He also purchased clothing from the Nebraska Clothing Company, a mail order business based in Omaha. In the fall of 1895, Bard purchased a suit of clothes from the Fish Brothers store in Chicago while on business in that city. [6]

Cowboys could cheaply obtain military clothing from soldiers or government surplus sales when available. Rollinson had a friend buy some blue wool army shirts and trousers from soldiers at Fort Boise, Idaho,

explaining that "Soldiers were generally broke, and always ready to sell their shirts and pants, which made excellent garments for a cowpuncher to wear."[7]

Cotton, wool, linen and silk were the principle fabrics available to the clothing industry during the period. Wool and cotton tended to be the most popular material for work clothing.

As in all clothing, styles in western men's work clothing changed over time. During the 1860s, unfitted, less tailored clothing dominated men's work fashions. It was not until the mid-1880s that tighter, tailored clothing began to appear, and remained in style into the early part of the twentieth century. Design elements distinguished particular brands, but essentially work clothing styles remained the same.

The cowboy wore clothes that were suited to his needs. During the 1860s and 1870s, the cowboy's coat, trousers, and vest were generally of the sort

← Planter's hat as shown in the 1878 Montgomery Ward & Company catalog. *[University of Wyoming, Coe Library]*

commonly purchased at the rude stores of the frontier. Made mostly of black or dark-colored wool, the coats and trousers were large and roomy. By the mid-1880s, mixed cloth and lighter colors came into wider use, but this was mainly because the storekeepers and mail order catalogs had such items for sale. In short, clothing was selected for comfort and convenience, for the cowboy was little dictated by fashion until the early 1920s.

⊰•◆•○•◆•⊱

HATS   Historic clothing catalogs show the evolution of the cowboy hat. One of the more well-known hat suppliers for the working class, beginning in the 1870s, was Montgomery Ward.

The only broad-brimmed hat available in the 1874 Montgomery Ward catalog was the "Men's Panama Hat" which was made of fur felt.[8] Four years later, in 1878, Wards added a new style of hat to its line called the "Men's Planter's Hat." This hat was made of either Saxony wool felt or Cassimere fur felt. The wool planter's hat was offered only in black, while the fur felt hat was sold in black, drab and slate.[9] The fact that Montgomery Ward carried a limited

This photograph was taken in 1889 at Evanston, Wyoming, after a riding contest between the "Bear River Boys" and the "Bridger Valley Riders." The contest was a tryout for Buffalo Bill's Wild West Show.

Bob Calvery is stretched in the foreground.

Front Row: Charles Byrnes, Jeff Edmondson, Will Stoll, Perry Allen, Oscar Quinn, George Hereford, Albert Burns, and Buckskin Joe Brown.

Middle Row: Gavin Barr, George Gill, Bob Hamilton, Willie Burns, Dick Jones, Gaird Butler (the Englishman), Eddie Burns, Tom Casto, Stephans, and the Ingersoll boy (partially cut off). Back Row: John Gill, Tom Anson, Tude Hereford, Ben Seaton, Herman Critterdon (foreman of the 100 outfit), Charles Hamilton, Bill Harvey, Cris Early, Allie Ingersoll, Charles Ingersoll. *[Sweetwater County Historical Museum, Green River, Wyoming]*

→ This unidentified cowboy was photographed near Newcastle, Wyoming, in 1892. He has a Stetson "Boss of the Plains" hat on his knee. Also note that he wears wrist cuffs. *[Anna Miller Museum, Newcastle, Wyoming]*

inventory of western style hats indicates that these hats were not popular for work during the early and late 1870s.

The lack of the western style hat in these catalogs also supports the supposition that, prior to the introduction of Stetson's hat, there were few broad-brimmed hat styles available that suited the needs of westerners. Floppy wide-brimmed wool felt hats and the planter's hat appear to have dominated the market for work hats in the midwest and northern plains during the early 1870s, while in the southwest the wide, stiff-brimmed, fine quality fur felt jaranos poblanos, imported from Puebla, Mexico, were popular for head protection. It was not until John B. Stetson developed his western style hat that the true cowboy hat began to emerge in all areas of the west.

Stetson is credited as the originator of the cowboy hat. Stetson was a hatter's son who was forced to move west from Philadelphia for his health. While residing in Colorado in the early 1860s, he conceived the basic design for his western style hat which he later called "The Boss of the Plains." In 1865, with his health improved, he returned to Philadelphia and began production of his western hat.[10] The original

↓ An original turn of the century Stetson's "Boss of the Plains" hat often worn by cowboys.

"Boss of the Plains" had a four-inch brim and four-inch crown, was "natural-colored" and weighed two ounces. Around the base of the hat crown was a leather strap for a band.[11] In the early 1870s, Stetson's hats were produced in only one grade of felt (two ounces) and sold for five dollars. The fall 1900 catalog from Sears, Roebuck and Company described Stetson's "Boss of the Plains" as the "most popular Cowboy Hat, made from the finest selected nutria fur. Silk band and binding; crown, 4½ inches; brim 4 inches; weight, 6 ounces." The only color offered was belly nutria and the cost was $4.50 plus postage.[12]

Stetson later made "The Boss" of finer felt that cost ten dollars and finally an extra fine fur made of nutria which sold for thirty dollars.[13] It was comfortable and distinctive in style, and the fur felt created a firm, stiff and durable brim. The name "Boss of the Plains" added a suggestion of swagger and command, which also contributed to the hat's success. The crown and brim of "The Boss" was not formed in the factory. Shaping was dependent upon the individual whim of the cowboy, who provided his own style of crease in the crown or roll in the brim. These early Stetson hats were lined with a beautiful crimson lining intended to shield the fur felt crown from perspiration.[14]

Stetson's hat utilized the fine qualities of the Mexican style sombrero adapted with a smaller brim for the windy northern plains region. This new style of hat became an almost immediate success, particularly among westerners and cowboys of the northern plains. In fact, "Stetson" became synonymous with the cowboy image. E. Hough states that a would-be "dude" cowboy would buy a cheap wool hat and be tormented by real cowboys:

He is pained and grieved to find that at the ranch he is derided for wearing a "wool hat,"

→ Stetson's "Dakota" style western hat. Note the "Montana Peak."

and he is still more discontented with his head covering when he finds that the first heavy rain has caused it to lop down and lose all its shape. The cowboy riding by his side wears a heavy white felt hat with a heavy leather band buckled about it, which perhaps he bought five years before at a cost of fifteen or twenty dollars; but he refers with pride to the fact that it is a "genuwine Stetson, an' a shore good un." [15]

The Stetson, after years of wear, did lose its stiffness and some cowboys punched holes in the outer edge of the brim, through which they laced a leather thong. This thong provided rigidity, preventing the brim from flopping in the wearer's face while he was riding or during windy weather. Some cowboys also used a leather thong which passed around the base of the crown and under the chin to keep the wind from blowing away their hats. [16] John R. Barrows, an early 1880s Montana cowboy, commented that the use of "two buckskin strings" to secure the cowboy's broad-brimmed hat was "common." [17] This may have been a common practice in Montana, but after examining hundreds of historic photographs of Wyoming cowboys, none show any evidence that this two-string modification was used in Wyoming.

By the end of the nineteenth century, shaping of hats became so popular in the west that Stetson began to create new styles with various crowns and brims. Each model or style received an appropriately western name: Austin, Bronco, Roundup, Dakota, Jarano Pollano and Columbia. [18]

Stetson was not the only hatter who supplied the cowboy hat. However, though many companies produced large-brimmed western style hats, "The Boss" was the most noted and desired by working cowboys. In 1895, Bob Fudge was swimming a herd of Texas

Roundup camp on the Big Red Ranch, Wyoming, 1898. The variety of shapes and styles of hats was a matter of personal preference as illustrated in this photo. *[Wyoming State Museum]*

→ The cowboy on the left in this 1903 photograph is wearing what appears to be a "Chief Moses" cowboy hat produced by Sears, Roebuck and Company. Cowboys could also purchase the red and silver stars to place on their hats from the same company. *[Wyoming State Museum]*

COPYRIGHTED
1903 BY
F.M. SHERMAN

cattle across the Platte River below old Fort Laramie when he was nearly drowned and lost his hat. Several of the cowboys working with him rode to Fort Laramie and bought him a "new Stetson" hat, size "seven and a quarter."[19] The Stetson was evidently important enough to risk re-crossing a swollen river to buy.

The success of Stetson and the increasing world interest in the cowboy undoubtedly influenced Montgomery Ward to offer its own selection of western style hats. In 1883, it entered into the market with several different styles of sombreros. These hats were made of either buckskin-colored or calfskin-colored fur felt and Saxony wool. The "Buckskin Sombrero" style was a "belly nutra or light fawn" colored hat that had four silver stars inlaid with fire red centers on the brim and two on the crown. It had a braided roll of silver woven cloth for the hat band and a satin lining with leather sweat band. These hats had a four-inch crown and five-inch brim. In 1900, Sears, Roebuck and Company also offered the "Chief Moses" hat with flaming red stars; they also sold the stars separately so that cowboys could attach them to their own hats.[20]

STETSON HATS

COL. McCOY

Made to order in any color or quality desired.
Dimensions: 9 inch crown, 6 inch brim

Prices:

White, Black or Tan, Clear Nutria.... $65.00
Select Beaver, Buckskin................. 75.00

Silk Lined

↳ The original ten gallon hat called the Colonel McCoy as produced by Max J. Meyers in 1925. *[Palen Collection, Cheyenne, Wyoming]*

Pratt & Ferris cowboys before leaving for the 1898 fall roundup near Lusk. Note the hunter's and Scotch style winter caps and winter coats.*[Wyoming State Museum]*

Montgomery Ward's Saxony wool felt hats came in "leather" and silver grey colors. The brims on these hats measured from 3½ to 5 inches wide with crowns from 3½ to 5 inches high, depending on the model.[21] These hats remained unchanged in Montgomery Ward catalogs until 1890, when for the first time the new styles were officially designated "Cow Boys' Hats." Also in 1890, Montgomery Ward hats were offered solely in fur felt with silk or leather hat bands. The brims averaged four to five inches and the crowns varied from 3½ to 6 inches high depending on the style.[22]

The next major style change in the Montgomery Ward catalog was in 1910, when the catalog carried its own hats as well as a selection of those made by the John B. Stetson Company. It is interesting that this catalog offered two styles of hats with high crowns. The first, "The Denver," had a curled 3½-inch brim and a 5½-inch crown. The second was called the "Big Four Hat" and sported a center crease, six-inch crown and a four-inch curled brim.[23]

The so-called ten gallon hat was not a traditional hat of the nineteenth century. It was developed in Cheyenne, Wyoming, by Max J. Meyers in 1925.

← The hats with the high crowns in this 1890s photograph appear to be "Ten Gallon" hats, but in fact they are not tall enough. Standing in the center back is John B. Kendrick. Charles Howell of Newcastle is the man wearing the sweater in the back who moved as the photograph was taken. *[Anna Miller Museum, Newcastle, Wyoming]*

← Often one man having the talent of a barber drew the lot of shaving the roundup cowboys. This photograph, taken in eastern Colorado on the Hugo Ranch in 1903, is typical of scenes from the Wyoming Range. *[Wyoming State Museum]*

The first ten gallon hat was produced for movie star Tim McCoy and sported a nine-inch crown and a six-inch brim. The Stetson company made this hat at the request of Meyers who then sold it to McCoy. The style achieved immediate success among movie stars and rodeo cowboys.[24]

For winter wear, there was a variety of caps available. The hunter's style wool or corduroy tie-top caps appear to have been the most popular among Wyoming's cowboys. The scotch cap is also conspicuous in historic photographs. Even so, these types of winter headgear only begin to appear in photographs of the late 1890s and after the turn of the century.

▸◂•◦◦•▸◂

HAIR Often misrepresented in movies and print was the length of a cowboy's hair. Joseph Mora states that longer hair was common in the 1860s and 1870s:

> Among the very early cowmen, the long hair was quite prevalent. This was not worn in a spirit of Wild West showmanship, as really happened in many cases later on after Buffalo Bill, Ned Buntline, and the lurid dime novels created a Wild West type for eastern consumption. In the ante bellum days, and those immediately following, the

trend in masculine coiffure was for long, hair. I do not mean that in all cases it had to drape over the shoulders, but it was for long, locks...on the frontier where a man might go for months and months without even an approach to a barber shop, long-hairs were not an uncommon note. Moustaches were the vogue, and the smooth face was the exception; and that generally due to extreme youth or the inability to raise one... Goatees were also quite popular, and, as a rule, cowboys looked older than they do today.[25]

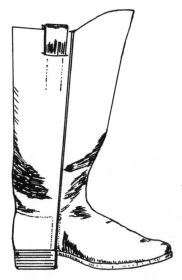

← These M 1872 U.S. Cavalry boots could be purchased through surplus or from soldiers down on their luck. *[Drawing by Lindmier from original photograph dated 1875, Smithsonian Institution]*

During the 1880s and later, hair tended to be cut short unless the cowboy was unable to find someone who could act as a barber or was unwilling to attempt the task himself. Rollins states that:

> ...long hair in itself was regarded as suggesting this purpose of screening, [the removal of the upper part of an ear on a horse thief] or else as indicating a desire to be in appearance though not in fact quite "tough and wild." Consequently, long hair did not meet with public approval.[26]

While out on the range or during a roundup, some cowboys acted as barbers for the other members of their crew. These men cut hair and shaved those who wanted this service. In the late 1880s,

← These early "granger" style boots belonged to "Big Nose" George Parrott. Parrott was a noted criminal who was hung near Rawlins, Wyoming, in 1881, but he was also a cowboy. Interestingly, Parrott's skin was tanned and made into a pair of shoes worn by Wyoming's first Democratic Governor, John Osborne, during his inauguration. *[Wyoming State Museum collection]*

↰ These stovepipe boots were popular during the mid-1870s. Note the reinforcement stitching on the uppers and the cloth webbing boot pulls. *[Wyoming State Museum collection]*

Floyd Bard provided this service while on a roundup near Buffalo, Wyoming. Bard explains:

> Three or four of the cowboys, once or twice a week, would get me to shave them or cut their hair. For Shaving, a cowboy would lay down on the ground with his head bent back over a rolled up bed. Down on my knees beside him I would lather his face and give him the shave of his life, which was about like pulling teeth.[27]

BOOTS Cowboys of the 1860s and the first part of the next decade utilized boots and shoes purchased off store shelves. Work shoes and boots of this time period were low heeled and broad in the toe, approximately 2 to 2 ½ inches wide. Work boots had wide tops and were usually higher in the front to cover the knee. They then sloped rearward to just below the knee. Construction was simple: wood-pegged or sewn soles were attached to one-piece, unlined leather uppers called vamps.

While most cowboys by the mid-1870s were wearing custom made cowboy boots, many Wyoming cowboys still purchased common over-the-counter work boots. Teddy Blue Abbott remembered that he had no money when he first became a cowboy in Nebraska in 1871. He said that his mother bought him his boots and that they "never wore out." Three or four years later, after wearing the same boots even though they were too small and hurt his feet, Abbott intentionally ruined the boots by standing too close to a fire so that his mother would have to buy him a new pair. When they went to town to buy the new boots, he tried them on first to ensure that they were "big enough." [28] These new boots were not cowboy boots but regular work boots.

Floyd Bard purchased his boots in 1892 from a grocery store in Buffalo, Wyoming. He remembered:

> Most all grocery stores handled some dry goods, especially foot wear, which came in big wooden boxes about four or five feet square. For men there was the granger boot, made from bull leather with broad toe and flat heels... The kids' boots were made granger style. This kind of footwear sold anywhere from two to four dollars. [29]

Government surplus also provided an economical outlet for well-built work shoes and boots. Montgomery Ward listed surplus United States government sewn boots in its 1874–1875 catalog. These

← Roy McCabe accompanied a Texas cattle herd into the Hulett, Wyoming, area during the 1880s. This photograph was taken to show his family how hard the trail drive had been on his clothing. Note his feet protruding from the boot toes. *[Sally Ann Neiman Collection, Hulett, Wyoming]*

→ This scallop-cut boot made of calf and Morrocco kid were custom made to fit and cost about $14 in the C.H. Hyer and Sons catalog. They featured a round box toe. *[catalog from the Joseph Palen collection, Cheyenne, Wyoming]*

CELEBRATED COWBOY BOOT MAKER
—3—

STYLE No. 70
Calf vamp and back Morrocco kid extended up above vamp and back; round box toe; wrinkled and stitched front; scalloped top.
Sewed $14.00
Pegged 13.50

ALL BOOTS CUSTOM MADE TO YOUR MEASURE

military boots were made of whole stock, white-oak tanned leather and were priced at $2.75 a pair. The catalog further described these boots as having a "broad sole, low heel; a comfortable and economical stogy boot." [30]

These boots worked well in the wide-sided wooden stirrup of the 1860s and early 1870s which did not allow the low-heeled boot to slip through. As stirrups became narrower in the mid-1870s, a higher heel was necessary to keep the cowboy's foot from pushing completely through when the rider was mounted. This need was met by the development of the cowboy boot.

As with all things, the cowboy boot evolved through the years. Each year a better design and construction technique was incorporated. On the early type of boot, the front of the heel aligned with the side welt of the upper. This created a weakness in design when the heel height was increased to two inches or more, as the soles were not well supported. To correct this problem, boot makers added a shank which kept the sole from collapsing. Through time they also discovered that the boot would fit more comfortably in the stirrup if the front of the heel was moved forward

→ This studio portrait of four Sweetwater County cowboys shows (seated) Tom Bailey and Billy Johnson. Standing are Tom Mariarity and Rox Avant. Billy Johnson wears stovepipe boots with fancy stitching. *[Fremont County Pioneer Museum]*

about three-quarters of an inch in front of the side seam. But this innovation did not happen until after the turn of the century, and this new heel design was not illustrated in catalogs until 1915.

By the mid-1870s, the stovepipe boot began to appear. Some of the stovepipe boots had a piece of red leather sewn over or above the boot top. Another variety of stovepipe boots had rows of stitching running from top to bottom on the uppers, which stiffened and strengthened the tops. Teddy Blue Abbott recalled his first cowboy boots, purchased in Nebraska in 1879: "They had colored tops, red and blue, with a half-moon and star on them."[31]

Another popular type of boot in the 1870s, called the kip boot, was merely a heavy work boot with uppers that came slightly below the knee in back and tapered up to knee high in front. The calf boot was a light leather boot, and the veal boot was a medium weight leather boot of similar design to the kip boot.

Boot top designs other than the stovepipe began to be popular in the late 1870s. Predominate among these was the scallop or "V" cut top which still appears on modern western boots. Additionally, two-piece

↙ This horse roundup crew was photographed near the Franklin Manke ranch in Converse County, Wyoming, in 1904. Some cowboys preferred to wear shoes rather than boots. Jim Williams (right forefront) wears lace-up work shoes. Seated: Clyde Griffis, Emer Smith, Jordan, Albert Herman, Fagan (by the wagon wheel), a boy who may be Jim Williams's son, an unidentified horse buyer wearing the bow tie, an unidentified man wearing the cap; P.N. " Pete" Summers with mustache, Frank Robison with the black hat, Jim Williams in front, Bob Jordan. Billy Blair is in back washing dishes and Fred Dale is standing with the bone. [*Wyoming Pioneer Memorial Museum*]

vamps began to replace the one-piece vamp by the early 1880s.

Another interesting feature was the pair of loops used for pulling on the boot. The earliest boots had web loops sewn onto the inside of the boot top either at the back or directly behind the side welts of the uppers. Later, both web and leather loops were used. The famous mule ear was another type of boot strap utilized during the latter half of the nineteenth century, but it is rarely seen among photographs of Wyoming cowboys.

By the early 1880s, fancy stitched uppers began to appear. The pattern stitched on the tops decorated the boot; but more importantly, the stitching increased the strength of the leather. During the late 1870s and into the 1880s, a slightly rounded and narrower toe became popular, but the two-inch tapered heel still remained.

In 1885, Montgomery Ward offered for the first time "Cow Boy's Boots" which were all calfskin boots with a fancy top, scalloped and stitched fifteen-inch leg and a two-inch heel.[32] This same type of boot was offered in a fancier model called the "Opera Boot" and differed from the Cow Boy's Boot in that a finer,

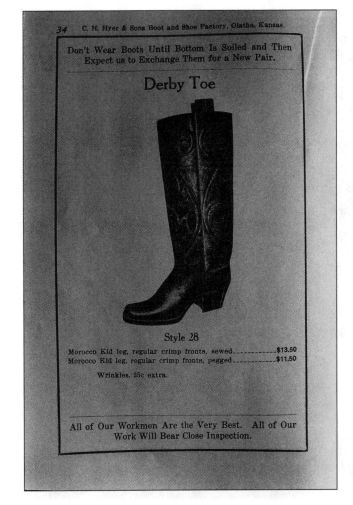

34 C. H. Hyer & Sons Boot and Shoe Factory, Olathe, Kansas.

Don't Wear Boots Until Bottom Is Soiled and Then Expect us to Exchange Them for a New Pair.

Derby Toe

Style 28

Morocco Kid leg, regular crimp fronts, sewed_____$13.50
Morocco Kid leg, regular crimp fronts, pegged_____$11.50

Wrinkles, 25c extra.

All of Our Workmen Are the Very Best. All of Our Work Will Bear Close Inspection.

← These stovepipe boots, illustrated in the C.H. Hyer and Sons boot catalog, had a derby toe and a Morocco kid leg. *[catalog from the Joseph Palen Collection, Cheyenne, Wyoming]*

⌐ In this 1903 photograph taken at the Hugo Ranch in eastern Colorado, the cowboy seated against the bedroll is "writing home." He is wearing Mule Ear strap boots. Note his sleeve garters and homemade hat band. *[Wyoming State Museum]*

kid-grade leather was utilized, along with more stitching. From 1885 until well after the turn of the century, Montgomery Ward catalogs showed an expanded inventory of cowboy boots, illustrating various styles.

Most early accounts, substantiated by historic photographs, indicate that the Wyoming cowboy wore the high-heeled, tight-fitting cowboy boot. Rollinson relates in the late 1890s:

> All the men were well shod in good-looking, riding boots, except the cook. I learned that the boots were mostly made by a bootmaker named Hyer, of Olathe, Kansas, and were generally black in color. All had seventeen-inch tops, with a two or two-and-a-half-inch heel, slanted well forward, so that the weight of the foot came well forward of the heel, and consequently the stirrup was held under the arch of the rider's instep, as it should be.[33]

Rollinson further discusses a procedure that the cowboys used to remove these tight boots:

> The men were tired, and a bunch of them had removed their boots to ease their feet. I was surprised to see one man back up to another on the ground who wanted to remove his boots

which were evidently too tight. His helper took the boot between his legs with one hand on the toe and one on the heel. The wearer of the boots put his free foot against the rump of his helper, and with much wiggling and twisting, the boot came off.[34]

It is difficult to determine the age of a historic photograph solely from the style of boots worn by the subject. Photographs and catalogs dating to the mid-1920s definitely show old-style cowboy boots among those of newer styles, indicating that the earlier styles were still desired by the working cowboy. By 1921, all the catalogs selling western wear exhibit only those boots with two piece vamps and fancy stitched uppers. The old fashioned stovepipe and kip boots were no longer available unless by special order through custom boot-making shops.

⊳·⊷·◦·⊶·⊲

TROUSERS During the 1870s and 1880s, four major fabrics were used in work clothing; wool, duck, corduroy and cotton jeaning (later referred to as denim). Wool trousers were originally considered the most durable for everyday ranch work, while duck and jeaning at first appeared best

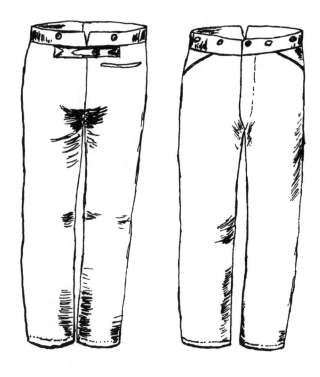

↶ Typical wool trousers of the 1880s. [U.S. Army, Uniforms and Equipment, 1889]

↳ 1870s and later style typical wool trousers. [U.S. Army, Uniforms and Equipment, 1889]

suited for (and preferred by) miners and farmers. By the end of the nineteenth century, historic photographs illustrate that canvas, duck, and denim trousers were becoming more popular, but wool trousers were still preferred. It was not until after 1890 that duck or denim trousers began to become more predominate for cowboys. As Philip Rollins put it, "Denim overalls were considered beneath the dignity of riders, and were left to wearing by the farmers, the townsfolk, and the subordinate employees of the ranches."[35]

Wool trousers of the latter half of the nineteenth century were of simple design and had no belt loops. Thus the waistband was tightened by means of a fixed belt adjustor and buckle in the rear of the trousers. Around the waistband were pairs of buttons near the top intended for affixing suspenders, and the front of the trousers opened by means of a buttoned fly. The legs evolved from a baggy appearance to a more tailored style as the nineteenth century came to a close. Most trousers had front pockets, and the cowboy preferred those that opened at the top rather than along the leg seam as this style prevented items from dropping out while mounted on horseback. Still, the cowboy had to purchase what fashion dictated and at times could not buy what he wanted.

Any number of colors and patterns were available in wool trousers. However, by the last half of the nineteenth century, most trouser wools were of a dark color and many had narrow pin-stripes running length-wise down the legs. Black and brown appear to have been the most popular colors with men of that era.

California pants, made in Oregon City, California, at the Oregon City Woolen Mills, were very popular among cowboys from the 1870s through the 1930s. Originally these trousers were fairly tight in the waist with loose fitting legs. They were made of heavyweight, thirty ounce, tightly woven pure virgin wool. Because they were pre-shrunk, they were almost waterproof. California pants came in a variety of colors including light buckskin and grey, with an interwoven plaid design.[36] As styles changed in the early 1900s, the fit of the California pants changed as well. During this period and later, these trousers were more baggy in both the waist and leg and also acquired belt loops.

↙ Taken from an original Levi Strauss letterhead, this illustration shows Levi Strauss's denim trousers of the 1873 pattern. *[Connie Lindmier Collection]*

Abbott refers to wearing "twelve dollar," light-gray California pants in 1885.[37] In 1884, Floyd Bard recalled his mother making clothes for the children in their family: "When these cowboys seen Mother making little suits for Tode and me out of discarded clothing, they started saving up their California pants, which were worn only in the seat."[38] Rollinson mentions Wyoming cowboys wearing California pants as late as 1898, substantiating their popularity well into the late 1890s.[39] Western clothing catalogs and western wear stores sold these pants as late as the 1950s.

Corduroy pants were also popular with cowboys during the late 1880s and well after the turn of the century. When John Rollinson became a cowboy in the late 1890s, his first pair of trousers were corduroy.[40] These trousers were of the narrow-waled or Sweet-Orr corduroy, and apparently the fabric was sturdy but the assembly was of poor quality. Shy Ousterhout explained that when a cowboy bought a pair of "sweetor" pants, he "had better get him a spool of tough linen thread and re-sew all the seams so they wouldn't pull out on him."[41] Corduroy trousers came in a variety of colors, but brown and light or dark drab were the most prevalent. As with

→ George Hodges and David Wilson, 1890s Newcastle, Wyoming, cowboys. Hodges is wearing California trousers and Wilson (right) has put cuffs on his Levi's 501 Jeans. *[Anna Miller Museum, Newcastle, Wyoming]*

the California pants, early corduroy trousers were tight fitting in the waist with baggy legs.[42] Their popularity was reflected in that they were shown in western clothing catalogs, such as the one published by Stockman-Farmer Supply Company in Denver, Colorado, as late as the 1940s.

Several companies produced canvas or denim trousers during the latter half of the nineteenth century and throughout the twentieth century. Carhartt began manufacturing tan canvas work clothing, including overalls, in 1889. Montgomery Ward began selling canvas, duck, or denim trousers as early as 1874. Yet the Levi Strauss Company is the most noted, and even today, denim trousers are generically called Levi's.

Levi Strauss began developing his heavyweight brown canvas overalls in 1853. They were waist high and straight-legged with only one pocket on the right rear. They could be tightened to fit at the waist by a belt adjustment on the back and had suspender buttons for attaching galluses for extra support. Once his initial supply of canvas was exhausted, Strauss switched to a material produced in Nimes, France, called serge de Nimes, which was later Americanized to the term denim. He selected a blue indigo dye to provide a uniform color for the denim and had the trousers sewn together with orange thread. These new blue trousers retained the same design as those produced of canvas.

In 1873, patented rivets were added to the pockets and seams of the jeans to provide strength. Front pockets were affixed and the arcuate design was stitched on the rear pocket. In the 1890s, these straight-legged, shrink-to-fit trousers were given a style lot number of 501. Belt loops were added in 1922, though suspender buttons remained until World War II. The next major change occurred in 1937 when the rivets on the rear pockets and the bottom of the fly were removed.

While these trousers were not popular among early day cowboys, they were gradually accepted by the early 1890s. Ed Lemmon, a cowboy from South Dakota and Wyoming, states:

I never saw northern cowpunchers or cowmen wear overalls or Levis. I worked with range cattle from 1870 to 1923, and I never wore overalls until I got my first flivver, about 1907, and then I wore bib overalls. No, the only cowhands I ever saw in overalls were a few who came up the trail from Texas. And they had started the drive wearing six-dollar California trousers, which on account of being made of such firm wool goods, wore out on the wrinkles. By the time they reached the first Kansas cow town some of them would have to make a change, and all they could get was overalls.[43]

Photographs of Wyoming cowboys indicate that while not totally common, overalls were in some use, especially in the 1890s.

By the 1920s, Levi's were in general use by Wyoming cowboys as they were long wearing and relatively inexpensive, costing about $2.00 a pair. At the same time, a new trouser entered the market, produced by Rodeo Brand wear. These "Rodeo Booger Reds" pants were made of a hard twisted duck, and were reddish brown in color. The two hip pockets and the two watch pockets featured corduroy flaps.[44]

SHIRTS Most work shirts between 1870 and the late 1890s were of the pullover style; that is, buttoning or lacing partly down the front. Although Floyd Bard recalled in 1890 that there was one cowboy working for the "76" ranch who almost always wore a red shirt,[45] the typical Wyoming cowboy wore a

← Note the various styles of shirts in this 1884 photo taken near Evanston, Wyoming. The man in the center is wearing a "lawn sports" shirt and lace up shoes. *[Wyoming State Museum]*

heavy woolen shirt of a dark or subdued color, especially during the winter. Wool shirts usually had roll-down collars that were permanently attached, and were normally worn closed to the top button. Most shirts between 1870 and 1910 either had no breast pockets or only one. However, there were some two-pocketed shirts, such as the 1883 dark blue wool flannel army shirts.[46] Some Wyoming cowboys wore the hickory shirt with its checked pattern, especially those who had trailed cattle from rural Texas to Wyoming.[47]

Cotton shirts shown in the historic photographs of Wyoming cowboys tend to be white or pin-striped dress shirts. It wasn't until after 1910 that these shirts came with permanently affixed collars. This style of shirt had a short collar that was closed with a stud and over which was to be placed a removable linen or celluloid collar. The removable collar could be of three varieties: standing, full fold over, or partially folded. Most cowboys wore these shirts buttoned fully to the neck, but they normally left off the collars. The cotton work shirts which were available differed from dress shirts in that they had attached collars. Cotton shirts are generally seen in photographs

← This 1893 branding scene is of unidentified Johnson County cowboys. Note the man wrestling the calf is wearing a fringed leather shirt and has slipped his suspenders off his shoulders for this task. *[University of Wyoming, American Heritage Center]*

↰ Two Cheyenne area cowboys remove shoes from a bronco around 1900. The man in the foreground is wearing Levi pants and a bib-front shirt. *[Fremont County Pioneer Museum]*

→ This photograph was taken in the 1870s before the men left on a cattle drive which ended in Wyoming. These men later cowboyed and took up ranching operations in Wyoming's Johnson County. Standing: Jack and Win Davis. Seated: John Tisdale, Al Allison, unknown. Tisdale was killed in the Johnson County Invasion. *[Tom Tisdale collection, Cheyenne, Wyoming]*

taken during the warmer seasons or when cowboys dressed up for studio photographs.

Bib-front shirts are also represented in historic photographs of Wyoming cowboys, but this type of shirt appears to be less than common, with bibs smaller than those common today. This style seldom appears in historic photographs prior to the late 1890s. Mail order catalogs, such as Montgomery Ward, Bloomingdale's, Sears and Roebuck, and E. Butterick, do not show bib-front or miner's style shirts until after the turn of the century.

In the Laramie, Wyoming, area, some cowboys wore buckskin shirts during the cold winters. Robert Mills was an English adventurer who desired to experience the wild west and, among other occupations, became a cowboy in 1881. He wrote that while working for the Balch and Bacon ranch in November 1881, a wet snow covered the cowboys, forcing them to search "in the snow for pants & boots & buckskin shirts." He also states that it was too hot in summer to "wear buckskin shirts, although 'chaparejos' as our leg wear is called, are indispensable."[48]

During the late 1890s, full button plackets on shirts appeared, although they were not frequently

← Robert Mills, from England, probably had this photo taken soon after he arrived in Laramie in 1881. Note the planter's style hat and the pin-striped shirt worn unbuttoned (uncommon for this time period). He is also wearing his revolver butt forward and early shotgun chaps. *[Courtesy of Vickie Mathew and the Wyoming State Museum]*

→ George Hereford, a cowboy from Fort Bridger, Wyoming, in 1884. Note the pin-striped shirt and "Boss of the Plains" Stetson hat as well as his gloves and what appears to be a 40 foot plus rawhide riata. *[Wyoming State Museum]*

illustrated in mail order or fashion catalogs and are rarely seen in historic photographs. By 1910, however, these shirts began to be more popular for dress and work.

The historic photographs illustrate that the predominate work shirt well into the 1920s was made of wool flannel and not cotton. Also, by 1921, clothing catalogs indicate that most shirts buttoned completely down the front and few pullover shirts remained on the market.

UNDERWEAR AND SOCKS   During the first half of the nineteenth century, shirts were considered undershirts. To be properly attired in this time period, a shirt was covered by a vest or coat. By 1880, a true undershirt, made of cotton or wool/cotton mix, became acceptable for wear beneath the shirt. These undershirts were collarless and loose fitting at the neck and had a full button or pull-over placket. The cuffs of this undergarment were of a stretch material and had no buttons to close the sleeves.

Men's underdrawers changed little from the 1860s until near 1880. At this time drawers were only waist high and were made of cotton, silk,

wool/silk mix, cotton/wool mix, knits or wool flannel. They were closed by three or four buttons on the front, had a tie-string on the rear for adjusting snugness, and some had strings at the ankle to insure that they would remain in place. The knit variety had elastic knit gatherings at the ankles on the underdrawers and at the sleeves on the undershirts. After 1880, most of the undershirts and drawers had elastic gatherings at the wrists or ankles.

There has been some misunderstanding concerning the existence of the red Union Suit during the 1880s. This is probably due to the "Scarlet Knit Drawers" and "Matching Undershirts" that came into existence immediately prior to 1880. These "Scarlet" underclothes remained in the Montgomery Ward catalog until after the turn of the century. The Union Suit, or combination one-piece suit, gained popularity near the beginning of the twentieth century.[49] This underwear was first advertised in the Montgomery Ward catalog in 1896. While it may have been introduced prior to that year, it is doubtful that the Union Suit had widespread popularity before that time. The Union Suit had advantages over two-piece underwear because traditional undershirts

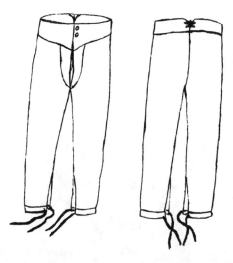

↙ 1870s style drawers. [Sketched from Secretary of War Reports, Quartermaster General Report, 1881.]

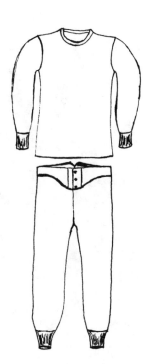

↓ Elastic two-piece underwear. [Sketched from U.S. Army, Uniforms and Equipment, 1889.]

tended to roll up the wearer's back and the drawers slipped uncomfortably. By combining the upper and lower parts together, these problems were avoided.

Until 1909, the Union Suit was made of various fabrics including Egyptian cotton, Lisle thread, knits, silk/wool blends and worsted wool. Depending on the type of fabric, the colors offered for these early Union Suits were light blue, natural gray, ecru and flesh.[50] It was not until 1909 that the Union Suit was

This photo of Converse County, Wyoming, cowboys was taken in the 1890s. Although one name seems to be missing, the cowboys are identified as Johnnie and Bob Howard, Everett Onyon, Sammy Covington, Bob Spaugh, Charles Bright, Ed Saffal, Billy Hanna, Oliver Lawrence and Charlie Moore. Nearly all of the men in this photograph are wearing vests. *[Wyoming Pioneer Memorial Museum, Douglas, Wyoming]*

→ Cheyenne, Wyoming, cowboys in 1882. Note that they are all wearing vests and all but one vest are collarless. Standing: Roy Robinson, Chris Abbott, William Ashby. Seated: Shocky Hall, Bartlett Richards, and John Harris. *[Wyoming State Museum]*

offered from Montgomery Ward in "pink," and this only in the mercerized silk/wool mix.[51]

Socks, made of wool, cotton or cotton/wool mix and available in various styles and colors, were an important part of a cowboy's underclothing. Ed Lemmon recalled that he shared a bedroll with someone else in order to have room in his war bag for extra socks. He felt that clean socks were important because:

...boots make sweaty feet, which bother a rider because he bears so much weight on them in the stirrups. When a man rolled out of bed at a quarter to three in the morning and didn't get back to the wagon until between seven or nine at night, he didn't feel much like hunting a mud puddle and washing out a pair of socks.... So all hands usually started the roundup season with several changes of socks, but along about the last two weeks they would all be used up. About then it got to be a custom to keep their eyes peeled for a newcomer into camp who might happen to have a fresh supply.[52]

>–•–◦–•–‹

VESTS As a point of fashion, vests were part of the outer clothing for men from the early 1820s on. Vests were originally called waist-coats and were

↳ Jim McMinneman on his horse Casey Jones. Photograph was taken near Spencer, Wyoming, in October 1911. McMinneman is wearing a sweater and woolie chaps. His rope is grass. [*Anna Miller Museum, Newcastle, Wyoming*]

intended to be worn under the dress coats of the period. Many Wyoming cowboys wore vests, but not necessarily because of fashion. Vests utilized by Wyoming cowboys were of two types: those with a collar and those without. Many vests were made with wool fronts and polished cotton backs and had from two to four small pockets. It was not until after the 1890s that calfskin vests gained some limited popularity.[53]

Since most early shirts did not have pockets, the vest pockets were of some importance. John Rollinson recalled, "Many of the riders wore vests, for a vest was most handy, in that it had pockets for tobacco, matches, and other nicknacks. The vest could be of any color and shade."[54] A vest was comfortable and allowed greater freedom of movement than a coat, and yet gave an added measure of warmth in cooler weather. Historic photographs show that many cowboys wore their vests unbuttoned. E. Hough explains:

> ...a vest closely buttoned about the body will cause you to perspire, so that you will quickly chill upon ceasing your exercise. His own waistcoat, loose and open, admits the air freely, so that the perspiration evaporates as rapidly as it forms. If the wind be blowing keenly when he dismounts to sit down upon the ground for

dinner, he buttons up his waistcoat and is warm. If it be very cold, he buttons also his coat.[55]

By utilizing the vest and coat, the cowboy used his body heat to keep warm while working and at rest.

>-⊷-○-⊰⊱-<

JACKETS AND SWEATERS The most common work coats for the entire nineteenth century were wool sack coats and morning coats. These jackets were generally purchased as part of a suit of the conventional Eastern style in shades of black, blue, brown or grey. While the styles changed little between 1850 and 1920, there were variations including the design of the collar, the shape of the skirt, and the length.[56]

Unless the weather was cold, the cowboy preferred not to wear a jacket, as it limited his mobility, especially while roping. Nonetheless, many of the photographs which show cowboys working illustrate that they did wear them when weather necessitated.

During cold weather, the Wyoming cowboy often wore a sweater, as this garment allowed more freedom of movement. Most of the sweaters were pullovers, but there were some similar to the turtle-neck type. Usually dark in color, many sweaters were

← Cowboys from the W.A. Carter ranch near Fort Bridger, Wyoming, in 1884. Left to right: Charley Charles, Bob Calvery (foreman), Eddie Byrne, Fletcher Kirkendall. Charles, Calvery and Byrne are all wearing morning coats. *[Wyoming State Museum]*

homemade by mothers or sweethearts, although Fort Laramie cowboy Jake Tonamichel was given his jersey sweater in 1885 as a Christmas present from older cowboys for whom he had wrangled horses.[57]

Coats and Gloves During the open range cattle era, there was little work for cowboys on the northern ranges during the winter months. Those few who were fortunate enough to be given employment usually rode line or did odd jobs about the main ranch. These cowboys needed protection from the elements, and a large variety of winter coats were available to them if they could afford the price out of their meager pay. Those who were able to purchase winter coats often bought the cheapest possible. Jake Tonamichel stated that he worked one winter with an outfit where "there was one overcoat in the whole outfit, and it was loaned around to his friends by the owner."[58] In contrast to Tonamichel, Teddy Blue Abbott was prepared for the winter of 1886-1887:

> I wore two pairs of wool socks, a pair of moccasins, a pair of Dutch socks that came up to the knees, a pair of government overshoes, two suits of heavy underwear, pants, over-alls, chaps and a big heavy shirt. I got a pair of woman's stockings and cut the feet out and made sleeves. I wore wool gloves, great big heavy mittens, a blanket-lined sour-dough overcoat and a big sealskin cap.[59]

Denim, duck and canvas coats with blanket linings were quite popular with the Wyoming cowboy. Shy Ousterhout related that his mother would reline this type of coat for cowboys.[60] Hough exemplified how common this type coat was:

> At times in the winter time, and in a colder country, the cowboy slips on a blanket coat, a long garment of heavy brown canvas lined with flannel.[61]

These types of coats, produced by various manufacturers including Carhartt, Montgomery Ward and J. C. Penney, were generally slightly longer than waist length. In 1886, Montgomery Ward produced its winter coat in brown duck and light or heavy weight jean. Both styles came with a canton flannel lining.[62]

Fur coats, such as those made of buffalo or raccoon, were generally too expensive for the working cowboy, but there were a few who managed to own them. In 1890, Jack Flagg wore a bearskin coat during the cold months near Buffalo, Wyoming.[63] Edgar Bronson made a ride during the winter of 1876–1877 in forty degree below zero weather. He kept warm as he rode, "bundled in arctics, goat-skin leggings, and buffalo overcoat, with a spare buffalo robe for my lap."[64]

Surplus military overcoats appeared in the Montgomery Ward catalog as early as 1874, but if near a military post, a cowboy might be able to buy an overcoat from a soldier who needed some extra money or who had deserted.[65] Teddy Blue Abbott stated that many of the cowboys trailing herds north from Texas were ex-Confederate soldiers, and they used their military overcoats as a combination coat, slicker and bed blanket.

Like the coats, gloves were varied in style and design. Unlike coats, however, gloves were not worn solely during the winter months or in cold weather. Cowboys wore gloves to protect their hands while working and nearly always when roping. Personal preference dictated whether they wore high quality buckskin gloves or fine leather gauntlets.

Few used gauntlets, according to Ben Bird, as they might become tangled when roping and "all sorts

← Joe Coslet, Al Allison and Tom Gardner are shown here wearing heavy fur coats in 1890 Johnson County, Wyoming. *[Tom Tisdale Collection, Cheyenne, Wyoming]*

← John B. Kendrick at the OW Ranch near Sheridan, Wyoming, in 1885. Kendrick is wearing a sack coat and leather gloves. His gear included a rifle in a scabbard and a grass rope. *[Wyoming State Museum]*

of stuff would get caught in them."[66] Yet Hough states that many cowboys wore gauntlets "made of the finest buckskin, which will not be injured by wetting. It will probably be tanned white and cut with a deep cuff or gauntlet, from which will hang a little fringe."[67]

During a fall roundup near Wheatland, Wyoming, in 1902, John Rollinson made reference while riding on a cool, moonless night as a nighthawk," that he was glad he "had gloves...and a warm coat."[68] Later in 1903, Rollinson also said that he would "pull on a pair of wool socks" over his buckskin gloves for added warmth during extremely cold weather.[69] Hough recalls that many cowboys used mittens in winter instead of gloves as these kept the hands warmer.

During the winter, when roping was not so often employed, the range rider might wear fur gloves or mittens with wool linings. It was all a matter of personal need.

Not only did hands need protection against the elements, so did the eyes. Becoming snow-blind was a painful experience which could leave a cowboy "bed laid" for weeks. To protect the eyes from the bright sun reflecting off winter snow, the cowboy often used a mixture called war paint. This concoction, made of lamp-black and coal oil, was placed on the cheeks under the eyes. The cowboy could also use black linings cut from coats or black neckerchiefs as a mask to cut the reflected light.[70]

>⊷⊶<

RAIN GEAR Charles Goodyear first patented his gum-rubber coated fabric in 1844. This black rubberized muslin was then made into water-resistant clothing, of which various styles of coats, ponchos and slickers were employed by the cowboy to ward off the elements. Even so, Teddy Blue Abbott states that the cowboy of the seventies "…had no tents, no tarps and damned few slickers."[71]

It wasn't until November 1881 that Abner J. Tower developed his Fish Brand mustard yellow Pommel Slicker.[72] This long coat was made from oil-cloth and was intended for the stockman, as it was split in back for use while riding or walking. With the original patent slicker, when on horseback, the cowboy and the pommel of the saddle were covered. Tower also made a black rubber rain coat, but it was said that the black color spooked the stock more than the yellow. During the fall roundup of 1902 near

⌐ This recreation of the patent office drawing of A.J. Tower's Pommel Slicker. shows the detail of the design. *[University of Wyoming Coe Library]*

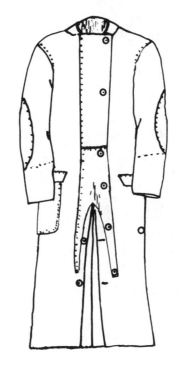

⌐ This drawing from the original patent office drawing of Tower's Pommel Slicker demonstrates how the front piece covered the pommel. *[University of Wyoming Coe Library]*

⌒ Dick Lamaureux near Lander, Wyoming in the 1890s. Note his beaded gauntlets, shirt sleeve garters and saddle pockets. *[Fremont County Pioneer Museum]*

Goshen Hole, John Rollinson noted that Tom Horn was riding for the Swan Land and Cattle Company's Two Bar roundup crew. On a cold rainy night, Horn visited Rollinson while he was riding night herd on the horse cavvy, and was wearing "a black slicker, which caused him to be scarcely visible."[73]

Tower's pommel slicker became so popular that other companies began copying his product. The 1885 Montgomery Ward catalog carried the Fish Brand slicker for the first time, but by the summer of 1886, it showed another brand called "Duck Brand, Yellow Oil Clothing." The only difference between the Fish and Duck slickers appears to be the name and the price. The Fish sold for $2.75 and the Duck sold for $2.30.[74] The A. J. Tower Company continued to produce its Fish Brand slicker until December 29, 1958, when the company went out of business.[75]

Changes were made to the original design through the years. The early patented slicker had a storm flap that covered the pommel of the saddle as well as the rider. In 1885, the slicker was improved so that it covered the rider and his saddle from front to back. The first models had a fall-down collar, but by 1885, a red wool stand-up collar appeared. These

⌐ Two cowboys at work on "Hard Winter" Davis's Spectacle Ranch in Johnson County,
Wyoming, during the 1890s. Note the cowboy on horseback is wearing a Fish Brand slicker.
[Tom Tisdale Collection, Cheyenne, Wyoming]

→ These cowboys are from the John Lee Ranch near Crowheart, Wyoming, in the early 1880s. Left to right: Will Lanigan, Ed Lanigan, Tom Tway, Jimmie Burroughs (wearing a slicker) and Dave Pichard. Jimmie Burroughs was found dead near Dubois and buried on July 2, 1892. The Lee ranch went out of business around 1891. *[Fremont County Pioneer Museum]*

pre-twentieth century slickers had one-inch diameter die-cast, zinc buttons, while later models marketed after 1911 had 7/8-inch diameter brass stud buttons and tan corduroy collars. Throughout the evolution of Tower's slicker, all models retained the mustard yellow oilskin or black rubber fabric.

The slicker was not used just to keep the weather off the cowboy. Floyd Bard used his slicker to secure a can of tomatoes to his saddle during the spring roundup of 1895 near Buffalo, Wyoming.[76] John Rollinson recalled that he tied his slicker over his horse and saddle while the horse was standing idle in the rain so that both would be kept dry.[77]

The early oilskin slicker was not ideal. While it served to keep the rider and his equipment dry, it was a poor substitute for an overcoat. As one Texas cowboy said, caught in a sudden storm, "If I'd had two of the damned things on I'd a-froze plumb to death."[78] In cold weather the slicker became stiff and made a crackling noise which spooked the horses. When tied to the saddle, the coat was draped across the back with as few folds as possible; if left folded for long periods of time, the slicker cracked along the folds. Finally, when hot, the slicker became sticky.

Nevertheless, the yellow slicker was the best thing available to protect the cowboy from wet weather.

><•>—O—<•><

DUSTERS & CAR COATS Unlike modern versions, historic men's dusters afforded limited protection and were intended to do just what the name implied: keep dust off a traveler's clothing. Museum samples of these light coats are consistent in their design, construction and fabric. Early dusters inspected in these collections are primarily single-breasted garments made of a light weight white or off-white linen with hard black rubber buttons. Most were not reinforced with a lining.

The Wyoming cowboy had little use for such a garment when traveling by horseback because of its limited protection against weather. Historic documents and photographs indicate that these linen coats were primarily intended for travel on stagecoaches, railroad cars, and later for use when traveling in early automobiles.

Some stagecoach companies provided dusters to each traveler when they boarded their coaches as a means of protecting their customers from the large amounts of dust generated on the long dirty wagon roads. Upon reaching their destination, travelers returned the dusters to the ticket agent. The stage coach company had the dusters cleaned and then they were reused.[79]

><•>—O—<•><

BANDANNAS Perhaps the most utilitarian article of clothing that a cowboy owned was his bandanna. It could be used as a dust screen during the summer and as a barrier against the cold in the winter. Joseph A. Spaugh was a cowboy with a trail herd bound for the northern territories in the 1870s. He tells how he used his bandanna on the long drive:

> It was burning hot on the plains and oh, that terrible alkali dust. I put my red cotton handkerchief up under my hat and let it hang down over my face to keep that awful dust out of my nose.[80]

A cowboy could tie his hat down over his ears with his bandanna during cold windy days, or use it to absorb sweat in extreme heat. John Rollinson, while riding nighthawk on a fall roundup, stated that "…some nights I wore a bandanna under my hat to protect my ears" from the cold.[81] Bandannas could be used to hold a hot cup or as a rag while working around a camp fire. They were equally practical for use as a bandage or to cover the eyes of a skittish horse while it was being saddled. Basically, the bandanna was a cloth of many uses, and it seems to have enjoyed nearly universal employment among cowboys.

Most bandannas were of cheap cotton or silk, and were either solid colors or printed. During the winter, cotton or wool flannel bandannas were often employed to provide better protection against the cold weather. According to Hough, most bandannas were "some bright colour, usually red, for these strong and barbarous natures have learned no admiration for the degenerate colours, such as pale green and the like." [82]

⋗—◦—⋖

SUSPENDERS & BELTS   Suspenders, or galluses, were used as personal needs dictated. Many an early Wyoming cowboy did not wear suspenders to keep his trousers up, but instead relied on a tight fit. Early accounts say that the cowboy scorned their use as restrictive and not fitting with the "cowboy image." Historic photographs of the early 1880s and later, however, indicate their common use. Rollinson recalled in the late 1890s:

Some of the men wore heavy leather belts and some went without a belt, while others wore suspenders. The belts were of various sorts. Some were of six-inch-wide webbing, with leather straps to the suspender buttons, and double buckles. [83]

These belts may have been the bucking belts which became popular at this time, especially for rodeo riders.

⋗—◦—⋖

WOMEN'S WEAR   There is little question that women assisted with a variety of work on early ranches. Wives, daughters, and sisters were often the only "hands" available to help the male operator of a small ranch. These women were left with all responsibility when the man of the family took an outside job, was injured or ill, or was off with his neighbors on a roundup or cattle drive. Still other women homesteaded independently or were left to run a ranch upon the death of a husband or father.

What these women wore while working is not well documented and is outside the scope of this book. Through the reproduction of postcards of the era, Judy Crandall's *Cowgirls, Early Images and*

↙ Group of cowboys on the 1910 roundup at North Paint Rock. Note the suspenders on some of the men. Front row, left to right: Ralph Mercer, Charles Kelly, Clarence H. Gardner, Bassill Kirkpatrick, Abe Goteval, Frank Robinson. Second row: Perk Davis, Dan Lee Morris, Jack Thomas, A.J. Church, J.S.F. Gapin, Ben Biesman. Third Row: Ed Williams, (cook), Ted Shaffer, Bert Allen, Fred Russell, Sam Wray, Bill Mayer, E.Y. Allen, T.F. (Tude) Nelson. *[Wyoming State Museum]*

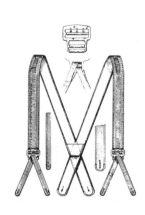

→ Typical suspenders of
the late nineteenth century.
[U.S. Army, Uniforms &
Equipment, 1889]

In this photo of a roundup crew taken around 1890 north
of Cheyenne, several men wear suspenders. Also note that a
number of the men wear vests. [Wyoming State Museum]

Mrs. Jack Elliott wore a split riding skirt in this 1920s photograph taken on the Chaulk Bluff Ranch near Cheyenne, Wyoming. *[Joseph Palen collection]*

Collectibles[84] provides excellent photographic documentation of what performing cowgirls wore from the 1900s to the 1940s. However, the silk and white buckskin of rodeo cowgirls and actresses can not be considered typical.

Split riding skirts can be seen in some early photographs. However it is suspected that for day-to-day work women combined traditional women's clothing with the portion of men's attire that they deemed most practical. Cowboy hats, chaps, boots, gloves, and bandannas could be worn by either sex. Shirts and trousers could be adapted. It seems likely that many women wore much the same clothing as their male counterparts when working with livestock or on the range.

CHAPTER THREE

RIDING GEAR

← Angora and early style batwing chaps adorn these Cheyenne, Wyoming, cowboys in 1907. Left to right: Dan Thompson, J.P. Coats, Jack Elliott and Floyd Carroll. *[Wyoming State Museum]*

CHAPS As the cowboy moved north into the mountains and plains, he brought with him many items of Spanish origin. Perhaps the most recognizable of these were his chaps. Pronounced "shaps," the term was an Anglicized derivative of *chaparejos.* Originally a part of the saddle, they were called armas (shield) and covered the horse's chest and neck as well as the rider's legs.[1]

By the 1870s, the garments had evolved into shotgun chaps, so-called because they were basically two leather cylinders resembling the barrels of a double-barreled shotgun. Also known as leggings, these early chaps were high waisted and cut square across the top. Each leg of the chaps was one piece of leather which wrapped around the cowboy's leg with leather lacings connecting the front and back of each leg on the outside. Generally these seams were further decorated with fringe, conchas or both. Pockets that closed with a flap were commonly found on the

Jim Kidd Willoughby in 1884 near Cheyenne, Wyoming, wore a pair of dark colored woolies. *[Wyoming State Museum]*

front of the upper thigh. The legs were sewn to a belt that laced together in front and buckled in the rear. Most of the waist belts were border stamped and some had minor floral carving or a basket weave design. On all early nineteenth-century chaps, the waist belts were square cut.

Teddy Blue Abbott recalled that many of the cowboys in the 1870s "had a pair of fullhide chaps, or leggings they called them then. They were good in the brush and wet weather, but in fine weather were left in the wagon."[2]

According to John Rollinson, turn of the century southeastern Wyoming cowboys seldom wore chaps, but in the Cody area they were common. He also stated that he "found they were a great help in riding, as leather clings to leather, and gives one a firmer seat in the saddle, and a stronger grip with the knees. In wet weather they were also admirable."[3] Harry Williams, a Big Horn Basin cowboy, noted that::

...chaps were and weren't worn. I seldom wore them, they were too unhandy. Of course when a rainstorm came up and I needed them, they were in the wagon. I wore out several pair just throwing them around.[4]

↑ Orin Porter and Bans Killborn, two Evanston, Wyoming, area cowboys in 1884, wearing their shotgun chaps. *[Wyoming State Museum]*

↑ Olof Benson in an 1890s photo. Location unknown. Note the 1875 Remington revolver. The shotgun chaps have no tie strings in front. *[Wyoming State Museum]*

↑ This 1920s photograph shows an unidentified woman from the Lander, Wyoming, area. She is well armed with two revolver belts above her woolie chaps. *[Fremont County Pioneer Museum]*

Shotguns chaps were put on like a pair of pants. The cowboy folded them in half, pocket to pocket, and then he could pull them on over his boots, even if he was wearing spurs. To remove them, the cowboy rotated the chaps on his legs (so that the pockets again touched) and then pulled them off. It is surprising that when this procedure was followed the cowboy did not have to remove either boots or spurs when donning or removing his shotgun chaps.

By the late 1880s, two more variations of chaps were introduced. The first was known as batwing or wing chaps. They closely resembled shotguns except that they buckled up the entire length of the outside leg seam. Rather than fringe, they had generous amounts of leather added to the outer leg. As they evolved, fewer buckles were used and the flapping leather legs became larger. The legs were often colored or had colored leather designs sewn on their extremities.

The second variation introduced in the early to mid 1880s was the Angora or woolie type. These chaps were primarily made from Angora goat skin, although they were also fabricated of bear skin. The early woolies were of solid colors, either natural

← Zack Jay and Paul Deford, Hulett, Wyoming, wear woolies. This photograph dates about 1916. *[Mrs. Sally Ann Neiman Collection, Hulett, Wyoming]*

← Two Lander, Wyoming, area cowboys, Dick Glover and F. Mann in about 1900. Both men are wearing woolies and Glover has beaded gauntlets. *[Fremont County Pioneer Museum]*

white, "old" gold or black.[5] Angoras had a canvas lining which helped in putting them on or removing them as the rough leather, opposite the fur side, would not slide easily over the cowboy's trousers. Woolie chaps were popular on the northern plains because of their added warmth. Rollinson wrote that in the Cody area, both leather and Angora goatskin chaps were in general use near the turn of the nineteenth century.[6]

During the last decade of the nineteenth century, basket or flower stamped belts for chaps became more common than the simple border stamp. As rodeos grew in popularity, flashier chaps made their debut. By the early 1920s, long shaggy, mottled or spotted colored Angoras were seen on the rodeo circuit.

Around 1910, the dip belt was introduced, on which the front of the belt halves curved downward. This added a great deal of comfort as the belt did not cut into the stomach while the cowboy was mounted.[7] The single thong or narrow buckled strap which connected the two legs along the top did not become popular until more recent times, when rodeo riders became concerned that the lacing would catch on the saddle horn, causing injury.

While today's modern shotgun chaps have zippers, they still bear a close resemblance to their predecessors. Modern rodeo batwings, however, with their wild colors and cuts, scarcely resemble the early wing chaps of the nineteenth century. Angora chaps are seldom used today by working cowboys and if used, are generally vintage chaps.

>+>–0–<+<

SPURS Spurs worn by the typical Wyoming cowboy during the late nineteenth century had two-inch or smaller rowels and commonly had up-turned hooks on the top of the rowel shanks. This hook was known as a chap guard and was intended to prevent the chaps from interfering with the rotation of the rowel. In some historic writings these hooks are referred to as bucking hooks. Supposedly, some cowboys hooked the protrusion into the saddle's cinch, thereby providing a better grip on a bucking horse. Research indicates that few if any cowboys applied chap guards for this purpose.

Some cowboys wore spurs with jingle bobs attached to the shank that the jingle bob swung freely against the rowel and chimed with the slightest movement. To keep the spur from rising on the boot,

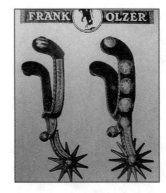

↑ Four common spur styles as sold by Gillette, Wyoming, saddler Frank Olzer in his 1905 catalog. *[Joseph Palen collection, Cheyenne, Wyoming]*

↑ Spur illustrations taken from the 1913 Hamely and Company catalog. These spurs have chap guards which were sometimes called "bucking hooks." *[Joseph Palen collection, Cheyenne, Wyoming]*

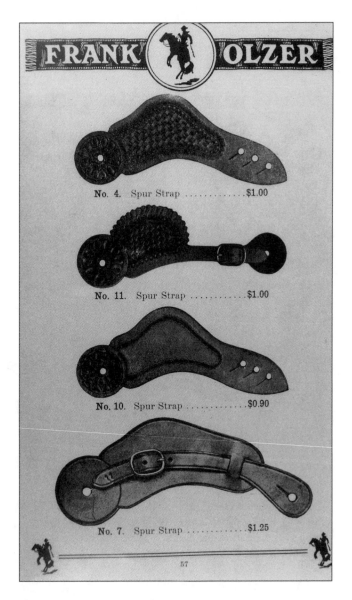

FRANK OLZER

No. 4. Spur Strap $1.00

No. 11. Spur Strap $1.00

No. 10. Spur Strap $0.90

No. 7. Spur Strap $1.25

57

→ Variety of spur leathers as offered by Frank Olzer in 1905. *[Joseph Palen collection, Cheyenne, Wyoming]*

heel chains were often used, though many spurs utilized a leather strap for this purpose instead.

Spurs were either made by a local blacksmith, bought through a saddle maker's catalog, or purchased at the local general mercantile store. John Barrows, a Montana cowboy who began his career in 1881, discussed the spurs familiar to him:

> The heavy hand-wrought spurs were serviceable as accelerators ...These spurs with their silver inlay and large silver conchas represented twenty-five hard earned dollars.[8]

Spur straps of the late nineteenth and early twentieth centuries were wide and often came with fancy designs or conchas. Traditionally they had border stamping, basket weave, or floral design tooling on the leather. Early straps generally were of two varieties. One, a two-piece strap and buckle, could be attached to the spur by two different methods. Some cowboys elected to wear the buckles to the inside of the boot, while others preferred to wear the buckle to the outside. By examining historic photographs, it is known that this was purely a matter of personal preference, as both techniques were widely employed.

→ Selection of quirts offered by R.T. Frazier, Pueblo, Colorado. *[Joseph Palen collection, Cheyenne, Wyoming]*

The other type of spur strap was the one-piece variety with slots that hooked over the spur button on each side of the spur. Removing the spur involved unhooking the strap from one of the buttons.

Spurs were a tool with only one useful function: to urge the cowboy's horse to a quick start. Spurs could also be misused by an ignorant horseman. Ed Lemmon explained:

> Fiction writers always advise clapping spurs to their mounts when wanting to get the top speed out of them. This is a mistake, because the harder spurs are used the less speed one gets. Clamping spurs to a horse causes it to press away from the rowels, and that naturally slows its speed. Spurs are only for signaling a quick start, as for cutting and roping, but not for speed.[9]

>−+−▶−+−●−+−◀−+−◁

QUIRTS Commonly seen hanging from the saddle horn or from a cowboy's wrist was a quirt. Quirts were braided from leather or rawhide and were generally no longer than three feet and normally loaded with lead shot. On the handle end was a wrist loop while at the opposite end were two straps known as poppers. The quirt was handy for convincing an unwilling horse or coaxing a little more from a hesitant one. Hough described the cowboy's quirt as:

> ...a short and heavy whip, made with a short stock less than a foot in length, and carrying a lash made of three or four heavy and loose thongs. The handle is a wooden stick, or sometimes a short iron rod, covered with braided leather, and a thong attaches the quirt to the wrist. The quirt is now made as a regular article of saddlery, but in the early days the cowboys often made their own quirt.[10]

Bud Cowan spent the winter of 1896 with Tom Horn in a winter camp on Powder River with cows that belonged to John Coble of Iron Mountain, Wyoming. To pass the long winter hours, they worked with leather: "Tom and I went into winter camp and broke horses and made rawhide ropes, quirts, and hackamores all that winter.[11]

Not every cowboy liked quirts. John Rollinson preferred not to use a quirt, because, as he explained, "I never used a quirt in riding, for the reason that it is in the way and hampers a man when roping."[12]

−+−▶−+−●−+−◀−+−◁

ROPES A real working cowboy referred to his rope as simply a rope, a catch rope, or a lariat. It

Hair Ropes......$2.50 to $5.00

Genuine Mexican Magney Ropes,
$2.00 to $4.00

Rawhide Rope.....35c per foot

Silk Manilla, 38 feet......$2.00
Silk Manilla, with hondo.. 2.25

Oiled Whale Line Rope, 38-ft..$1.75
Oiled Whale Line, with hondo. 2.00

→ Frank Olzer offered this large variety of ropes in 1905. *[Joseph Palen collection, Cheyenne, Wyoming]*

seems that the Wyoming cowboy seldom referred to his rope as a lasso.

Then, as today, ropers varied in skill, with a good roper considered a highly valued addition to the ranch or roundup. Roping was used in all forms of range and ranch work, including branding and doctoring the cattle.

As the Mexican vaquero evolved into the American cowboy, his roping techniques underwent changes as well. Very early vaqueros used a rope made of hair from horses' tails. This rope was called a mecate.[13] While the cowboy did not use a mecate for roping, he did use one as a lead rope and rein combination in conjunction with the hackamore. The name mecate was later Anglicized to MacCarty. Ropes were also made of linen and cotton, but their use was infrequent in Wyoming.

In the evolution of ropes, the maguey rope was the forefather of the hemp rope and was favored by many Texas cowboys. David Dary describes maguey rope fibers as:

...extra hard. It holds a big, wide loop and throws very fast. But maguey becomes stiff as a poker in damp weather and breaks easily if tied hard and fast. Vaqueros and cowboys used maguey lariats only in dry climates and for light work, where many believed it was the best rope available.[14]

La reata, which roughly means "re-tie," is a rawhide rope still used by vaqueros today.[15] These ropes came in two styles: twisted like a grass rope or braided. They were generally ⅜, ⁷⁄₁₆, or ¼ inch in diameter and varied in length, usually fifty feet or longer. Vaqueros were quite skilled in a variety of roping techniques; however, due to the reata's inability to take a hard impact, such as a calf coming to the end of the rope, vaqueros dallied. Originally the term was *dar la vuelta,* which in Spanish means "to turn over and over." In using a reata, the dally is made allowing approximately one foot of the rope to spin on the saddle horn. For this reason, a large saddle horn was needed.

Many Wyoming cowboys, especially those who migrated from Texas, used the hard and fast method of roping. But Rollinson says that in the mountainous areas of the Big Horns, the cowboys generally used the dally. This was a safety measure as the cow might run on one side of a tree and the horse on the other.[16]

← Billy Cramer won the bronc riding title at Cheyenne Frontier Days in 1899 when this photograph was taken. *[Wyoming State Museum]*

→ Tom Casto and Cecil
Davis near Robertson,
Wyoming, in the 1890s.
Both men have grass ropes
tied to their saddles.
[Wyoming State Museum]

John Barrows discussed the methods used in making rawhide ropes and their shortfalls:

The standard rope was of braided rawhide, fifty feet in length, with a diameter of seven-sixteenths of an inch. It was the product of home industry. A selected part of the hide of a two-year-old beef was soaked for a few days in water to which wood ashes had been added. Then four long strips, half an inch wide were cut, and stretched under equal tension to dry. When dry, the hair was scraped off with a sharp knife, and the stretched strands, now of uneven width, were trimmed uniformly. The strands were now rolled up and soaked again for another stretching, after which they were again trimmed for uniformity. This was followed by a careful trimming of the corners, and the finished strand with its pointed oval section was perhaps three-eighths of an inch wide and one-sixteenth of an inch thick. The four strands, moistened for flexibility, were easily braided into a single rope, approximately round and of the desired length. In its rope form, following another soaking, and stretching, it was trimmed where necessary with a sharp knife and sandpapered for smoothness, after which it was thoroughly greased with beef suet and reduced to reasonable flexibility by

↑ These two cowboys, photographed near Sheridan, Wyoming, in 1891, have grass ropes tied to their saddles. The front rider has shotgun chaps and a slicker tied to his saddle. The man in the rear wears woolie chaps. *[Anna Miller Museum, Newcastle, Wyoming]*

drawing it through holes bored in a post or log. The loop end was provided with a rawhide "honda" or eye and the strands at the other end were secured so that they would not unbraid. The finished product was a rope, strong, not too limber, heavy in proportion to its bulk, and, best of all, maintaining those qualities so that the adept was not compelled to change his technique from day to day, as was the case if he relied upon a manila or sisal rope. The only objection to the rawhide lasso was its temperamental susceptibility to moisture. It could not be used in rainy weather.[17]

Many Texas cowboys brought reatas into Wyoming with them. However, Texas cowboys were already using the hard and fast method of attaching the rope to the saddle horn when they arrived in Wyoming. This method required a rope which could withstand the shocks and jerks of being tied to the saddle horn without any play in the rope.

The Plymouth Cordage Company provided such a rope. Established in 1824, the company originally used American hemp for its ropes, but manila replaced hemp in 1830 and proved superior.[18] Manila rope was economical and came in rolls sold by the foot.[19] The rope was cut to length and either a honda knot was tied or a factory honda was added. After the honda was tied, the rope was stretched, the hairs burned off and then it was waxed. Ed Lemmon utilized a manila rope in the late 1880s while catching a twelve-hundred-pound black stallion. He remembered:

> ...I decided to try a throw at him with my 7-16 Manila saddle rope. I made a dash in between him and his band and tossed my loop. When he tried to pass me, I swung in beside him and put my horse in motion to relieve the strain when the rope tightened on his windpipe. But before the loop had hardly closed on the stallion's neck he came at me like a charging bull, squealing, in rage, his teeth bared.[20]

The manila rope reacted to changes in weather so the cowboy would bring his rope into the bunkhouse to prevent if from getting cold and damp, as a damp hemp rope was difficult to work.

Most Wyoming cowboys in the latter half of the nineteenth century tied hard and fast when roping. While not absolutely necessary in securing the saddle to the horse's back, double rigged saddles were preferred by cowboys in Wyoming. This remained the norm until the turn of the century when

No 6 "COW BOY"

← This unidentified Chugwater, Wyoming, cowboy is wearing a colt revolver and carries a rawhide lariat in this 1884 photograph. *[Wyoming State Museum]*

Wyoming cowboys began to dally instead of tying the rope fast. In the first half of the twentieth century, single rig saddles of the Oregon or California styles began to dominate the plains and mountain areas of Wyoming.

LEATHER CUFFS Cuffs were leather wrist gauntlets presumably used to protect the cowboy from rope burns. A study of historic photographs and written accounts indicates that these items were developed sometime in the late 1880s but did not become very popular until the 1890s. In fact, since it is unsure what their practical purpose was, cuffs may have been merely a fashion trend. Surviving examples indicate that early varieties laced and buckled on the wrists while twentieth century cuffs generally had snaps.

FIREARMS The cowboy's firearms have been well documented. Thanks to the motion picture industry, the Colt .45 and Winchester model '92 are probably two of the most famous firearms in the world. While many other arms and models were available to the cowboy, the most popular sidearm was the Colt Single Action Army or Peacemaker revolver, first

← The four Georges of the Carter Cattle Company at Fort Bridger, Wyoming, in the 1880s wear various types of revolvers, gun belts and holsters. George Soleman, George Finch, George Hereford, George Barr. *[Sweetwater County Museum]*

introduced in 1873. When first offered, this revolver came with a seven-and-one-half-inch barrel and was chambered for the .45 caliber Long Colt cartridge. Later, several shorter barrel lengths could be obtained and a variety of calibers were introduced. While the .45 caliber proved to be the most popular, the .44 WCF (Winchester Center-fire), was nearly as prevalent.

The Colt revolver is constantly mentioned in the historic accounts of the cowboy in the American West. In 1903, John Rollinson had this to say about the cowboy's sidearm:

> We all carried guns. I remember that each of the six men had guns almost exactly alike. We all pre-ferred the Colt single-action six-shooter. Some liked the Bisley model, others the Frontier model. Some were of a different caliber, but all were built on a .45 caliber frame. I noticed that these men carried their guns with one empty shell in the cylin-der, and five loaded cartridges. This was for safe-ty's sake. The gun was carried with the hammer on the empty shell, and, when cocked, a loaded shell was ready to fire. [21]

Edgar Bronson recalled the revolver he carried when he arrived in Cheyenne, Wyoming Territory, in 1875:

Before leaving the train, I had prudently strapped to my waist a new (how distressingly new) .45 Colt's six-shooter, that looked and felt a yard long.[22]

John Barrows said:

In the early years of my Montana experience nearly every man and boy was armed for protection against the Indians ...Cowboys and men who were much in the saddle usually contented themselves with the favorite navy revolver, Colt's .45, the "peacemaker," serviceable, accurate, and powerful. This was loosely housed in a heavy, open-top leather scabbard, looped upon a cartridge belt...[23]

Virtually every historic photograph of nineteenth-century ranching shows working cowboys wearing sidearms. The only exception seems to be when working in a corral; but even then, the revolver is still worn by some of the men.

Historic accounts also testify as to the cowboy's proficiency with his sidearm, and they substantiate the fact that he practiced regularly. John Rollinson recalled:

Pete Steckels was probably sixty years of age ...He had a crippled hand from a gunshot wound and he walked with a limp from a bullet ...One

↶ These five revolvers were commonly used by cowboys on the Northern Plains. Clockwise from bottom: M1860 "Army" Colt; M1873 Colt manufactured after 1895; M1873 Colt manufactured before 1895; Colt double-action "Lightning"; and M1895 Colt "Bisely." *[Wyoming Pioneer Memorial Museum]*

→ Converse County area, Wyoming, cowboy Lee Moore, in 1883. Note that Moore is wearing a vest and has his revolver holster in "a cross draw" position.
[Wyoming Pioneer Memorial Museum, Douglas, Wyoming]

day while we were at Chug, shipping beef, a couple of us were shooting at a target out back of the railroad station some distance from the cattle. Hearing the shooting, Pete rode out where we were taking turns firing at a gallon bucket on a low post, about fifty yards away. He watched us awhile as we would draw and fire as quickly as possible. We could hit the can by slow aiming, but missed it when we fired from a quick draw.

Pete grinned and said, "Boys, try doing that draw this way: As the hand comes up from the holster or belt, with the gun, the thumb cocks it. Continue to raise the gun to the level of the eye — but not too close to the eye — and as the gun levels to the target, squeeze — don't jerk — the trigger," and without changing his position on his horse, continued, "see — like this," and almost before our eyes could follow his lightning like move, the gallon can jumped off the post at the report of his gun. His horse did not even flinch or step back.

We looked at him in amazement, and asked him to do it again, but he only laughed, and remarked, as he rode away, "You Boys will soon learn to do it. You know, practice makes perfect." Later I did learn that Pete's manner of drawing and firing was the faster way, and I

always used it. It saved a fraction of a second—
and seconds were what counted in the days
when gun-toting was popular.[24]

In 1896, Floyd Bard sold a horse to buy ammunition so that he could practice shooting with a .45
caliber revolver. He also referred to the revolver as:

...my friend. There was something about that
old forty-five that I liked. I most always took her
with me out into the hills. Never knew when she
might come in handy. She put me on an equal
footing with all kinds of problems. Most of the
rangemen had a six-shooter of some kind.[25]

Abbott reflected that cowboys always carried
sidearms, especially during the 1870s and 1880s
when life on the American plains was uncertain and
rugged. But as to cowboys wearing two revolvers, he
was adamant:

I punched cows from '71 on, and I never yet saw
a cowboy with two guns. I mean two six-shooters. Wild Bill carried two guns and so did some
of those other city marshals, like Bat Masterson,
but they were professional gunmen themselves,
not cowpunchers. The others that carried two
guns were Wes Hardin and Bill Longley and Clay
Allison and them desperadoes. But a cowboy with

⌒ Joe LeFors, cowboy turned peace officer, had this photo-
graph taken during the 1880s in Wheatland, Wyoming.
LeFors is wearing a morning coat and a Colt revolver.
[Wyoming Pioneer Memorial Museum, Douglas, Wyoming]

→ An unidentified cowboy from the Fort Fetterman, Wyoming, area. Note his long hair and that he carries two Colt revolvers which was very uncommon for cowboys during the 1880s-1890s. *[Wyoming Pioneer Memorial Museum]*

two guns is all movie stuff, and so is this business of a gun on each hip. The kind of fellows that did carry two would carry one in the scabbard and a hide-out gun down under their arm.[26]

Ed Lemmon recalled some cowboys carrying two revolvers but never saw "…a two-six-shooter man who could use both at once and be accurate. Many could use first one and then the other, but not both at once."[27]

The cowboy preferred a heavy caliber, generally no smaller than .41 caliber for his revolver. Favored revolvers, other than the Colt Peacemaker, included the M1851 and M1860 Colt, cartridge conversion of the M1851 and M1860, Colt Bisley, Remington M1875 revolver, 1858 Remington cartridge conversions, Merwyn and Hulbert, and the Smith and Wesson revolvers.

Also introduced in the same year as the Colt Peacemaker was the Winchester model 1873 rifle and carbine. This was the first lever action rifle chambered for a center-fire metallic cartridge.[28] Its predecessors, the Henry and the model 1866 Winchester rifle or carbine, used a rim-fire cartridge. The M1873 cartridge was .44 WCF caliber and was initially

→ Isom Dart was a cowboy and horse thief from the Sweet-water County, Wyoming, area in the 1880s. He was later killed by Tom Horn. Dart is wearing a revolver and an unidentified pistol. *[Sweetwater County Museum]*

intended solely for the Winchester rifle. But Colt began chambering their revolvers for the Winchester ammunition. This allowed the same ammunition to be used in both weapons, and this became a very popular combination.[29]

Common rifles and carbines included the Henry .44 caliber rifle, the Marlin lever action, Sharps breech-loading, Colt, Savage, the military-produced Springfield in both .50 and .45 caliber, the M1866 Winchester, and Winchesters of the following models: 1873, 1876, 1886, 1892, 1894 and 1895.

John Barrows recalled that many different types of rifles were carried by cowboys, especially during hunting trips:

> The hunter was variously armed according to special preference or the character of his game. The muzzle-loading rifle had been retired and in its place could be found the Winchester rifles '73 and '76 as well as their prototype, the Henry. The single-shot rifles, commonly favored for heavy game were Sharp's "Old Reliable," the "Ballard," and the Springfield "needle gun."[30]

In 1879, Cowan recalled that his father's rifle was a .45–70 caliber model 1876 Winchester. Living

↳ These rifles were all used by Wyoming cowboys. From top: Sporterized Spencer, Sharps carbine, M1873 Winchester, M1886 Winchester with "Nate Champion" stamped on the barrel, and a Remington-Keene which was owned by Nick Ray. Nate Champion and Nick Ray were both killed in the Johnson County War. *[Wyoming Pioneer Memorial Museum]*

near Laramie, Wyoming, his father used this rifle to protect his family and property from Indians.[31]

If needed, the cowboy carried his sidearm and rifle while he worked. In writing of his experiences as a tenderfoot cowboy in 1877 Wyoming, Edgar Bronson had a disagreement with his foreman which nearly resulted in gun-play. His friend Tex came to his aid and averted trouble by discreetly displaying his Winchester rifle. He wrote:

> ...to see old Tex idly sitting his horse seventy-five yards away, his .44 Winchester plainly loosened and partly drawn from the scabbard, his right hand caressing the stock...[32]

Bronson also had an experience in 1876 in which rifles came into play. He and eight cowboys brought a herd of cattle from Utah into Wyoming. Bronson owned the cattle and was acting as his own foreman. As the cattle drive advanced across Wyoming, several of the cowboys working for him became quarrelsome. Bronson recalled that one of the disgruntled cowboys "...was coming from the wagon with my rifle ...Just as I hit the ground, I saw him throw a cartridge into the great .45-120 Sharps, and cock it."[33] Later on, during the same cattle drive, his crew

RIDING GEAR ← 101

decided to revolt. He states that they all were:

> ...doubly armed, with a Winchester and six-shooter. Four were reckless enough to throw lead if they felt they ought to, and two were mean enough, I well knew, to welcome the chance, both with notches on their guns unfairly won by "getting the drop."[34]

During the 1870s and 1880s, firearms (both rifle and revolver) were carried. If the rifle was not in a scabbard on the saddle, it was in the chuck wagon or bed wagon. Barrows recalled an Indian scare while out working cattle on a roundup in 1883:

> The company carbines with their scabbards and ammunition were distributed, saddles were thrown upon our long distance horses and while Johnny threw a small supply of provisions into his yawning cupboard, his horses were hooked up and we galloped down the valley in a cloud of dust.[35]

By the late 1880s the Indian scare was over, but the range wars were beginning, and as Rollinson explains:

> In 1891, at every small settlement and post-office hitching rail in Wyoming, saddle ponies stood with a Winchester carbine in the scabbard. Every gun, whether a rifle or carbine, and regardless of

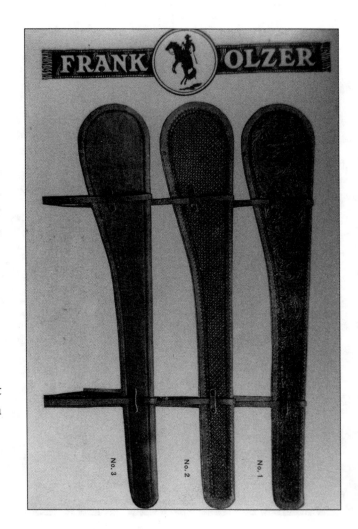

← Typical rifle scabbards from the Frank Olzer catalog, 1905. *[Joseph Palen collection, Cheyenne, Wyoming]*

⌣ These 1890s cowboys are branding a colt on the 76 ranch in Converse County, Wyoming. Note that two of these men are wearing their revolvers while involved in their work. *[Wyoming Pioneer Memorial Museum, Douglas, Wyoming]*

make, was referred to as a "Winchester." As a matter of fact, the weapon may have been a Marlin, Savage, or any other make of arm.[36]

Rollins states that except during troublesome situations like the "Powder River Invasion" or when the cowboy was hunting, the rifle was never carried. When carrying a rifle, it was conveyed in a "quiver-shaped, open-mouthed scabbard" attached to the saddle.[37] This rifle scabbard sometimes hung from the saddle horn by long adjustable straps,

...but more commonly was slung, butt forward, in an approximately horizontal position along the near side of the animal, and passed between the two leaves of the stirrup-leather. The rifle was thus eschewed, because, being heavy, it interfered with ready saddling and unsaddling; and, being bulky, it materially detracted from the rider's comfort.[38]

Toward the end of the nineteenth century, the carrying of sidearms became less popular and many cowboys began to leave their weapons in the ranch house. Harry Williams stated that he "seldom carried a gun, the lack of one saved me a heap of trouble. The later cowboy packed a gun because he wanted to be wild."[39] Hough adds that "Later on, say in 1887,

on some of the ranges got so wild as the far Southwestern country, there was slowly growing a sentiment against the wearing of a gun."[40]

Teddy Blue Abbott agreed that carrying sidearms became less popular during the 1890s. He explained:

...The country was getting so thickly settled then and the houses was so close together they figured they didn't need them any more.

But I wouldn't give mine up. A six-shooter's an awful lot of company. Suppose you break your leg, you can signal. If you're caught afoot you can shoot a jack rabbit. If you're held up you can defend yourself.

And then, too, six-shooters were a great thing for keeping the peace. You wouldn't have any of this calling names and brawling and fighting, where every man was wearing a deadly weapon in plain sight. And as for that expression about a son of a b., I never heard it said with a smile, as they say, before the nineties. In the early days men were soft-spoken and respectful to each other, because it didn't pay to be anything else. It's not like that now. But we were a prehistoric race. We were way behind.[41]

It cannot be denied that firearms, especially revolvers, played an important role in the life of the

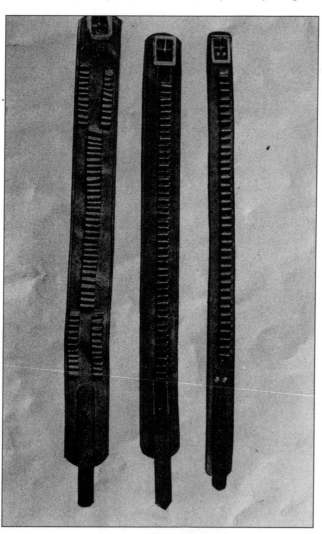

↳ Common revolver ammunition belts from the 1907 R.T. Frazier catalog. *[Joseph Palen collection, Cheyenne, Wyoming]*

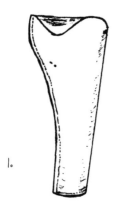

↑ Revolver holsters. 1. 1860s and 1870s style holster. 2. 1880s single loop holster. *[Authors drawing]*

Wyoming cowboy during the latter half of the nineteenth century and the early twentieth century.

⊷⊶

HOLSTERS & BELTS A wide variety of makers provided many styles of holsters and cartridge belts to the cowboy. Most of the holsters and belts were made by saddle makers such as F. A. Meanea, J. S. Collins and R. T. Frazier; but a few, especially those dating to the 1860s and early 1870s, were homemade. Edgar Bronson came to Cheyenne in the early 1880s to become a cowboy. Before leaving for the ranch he acquired more appropriate clothing and a new updated holster for his Colt revolver, which he purchased at Meanea Saddlery: "…even the pistol had to be stripped of its flap holster and rehabited in the then-new decollete 'Olive' scabbard." [42]

In 1882, John Barrows helped deliver a trainload of Montana beef to Chicago. While waiting for the return trip to Montana, Barrows decided to have a holster made for his Colt .45 Peacemaker revolver. He entered the Great Western Leather Works where

I found myself outside a broad-topped railing in a large room filled with industrious, pallid workers of both sexes. To the manager I explained my requirements, showing him the weapon and its worn holster. He seemed very much interested, as did his foreman, two or three callers, and as many operatives as could find excuse for leaving their work and coming to the front. But I noted the interest seemed centered in my pearl-handled pistol, and when I left the place, defeated and discouraged, it was after the discovery that the "Great Western Leather Works" confined its activities to the manufacture of ladies' purses and other hen-skin products.[43]

Holsters in the 1870s were open-topped and generally had a belt loop sewn on the backside which slid over the cartridge belt. Holsters of the 1880s and later tended to be made of one piece of leather with a back that looped over the belt and slots cut in the back through which the holster proper slipped. Most holsters for both periods came in natural or brown colored leather, although some were black.

The majority of these holsters had simple border edging while some of the fancier models were decorated with a basket weave design. Some were stamped with the initials of the owner or a ranch's brand, but none of the examples examined or viewed in historic photographs were carved.

All of the revolver holsters designed to be worn on the waist during the nineteenth century were made to slide on a belt. The combination holster and cartridge belt seen in movies did not come into use until sometime after 1910.[44]

Shoulder holsters were also convenient for carrying revolvers. They were supported by the shoulder with the revolver hanging below the armpit on the chest. John Tisdale carried his revolver in such a holster during the fall 1890 roundup in Johnson county. Floyd Bard was surprised when "Tisdale pulled his six-shooter from the shoulder scabbard from under his vest and began shooting coyotes."[45] The advantages of this type of scabbard were that it was easy to draw from while mounted or sitting and that it could be kept out of the weather under a coat or vest.

Most holsters used by Wyoming cowboys were supported on the waist by means of a belt. If the revolver was a cap and ball, this was a simple waist belt on which cartridge and cap boxes were carried along with the holster. After cartridge revolvers began replacing the cap and ball variety, looped cartridge belts were developed. These were usually made of pliable calf leather, doubled over and sewn along one

↑ 3. 1880s double loop holster. 4. Shoulder holster. *[Author's drawing]*

→ Folding blade pocket knives were often carried by cowboys. This illustration is typical of models available from several companies.

edge, producing a belt three to four inches wide. Medium sized silver or nickel-plated buckles fastened the belt around the waist. Sometimes these hollow-formed straps were used as money belts in which the cowboy could stash large sums of cash. In 1883, Teddy Blue Abbott "had seven hundred dollars on me, in my six-shooter belt" while visiting a theatre in Miles City, Montana.[46]

The number of loops on the cartridge belt was dependent upon the caliber of the revolver and the length of the belt, with most carrying between forty and fifty loops. Ammunition came in boxes of fifty; one box could generally fill the belt and the revolver. The total weight of the affair, revolver and ammunition, was several pounds.

⊱────◦────⊰

KNIVES Though the knife is often overlooked as an important tool of the cowboy, it had many uses. During branding, the knife worked for earmarking, castrating and making wattles or dewlaps. When doctoring cattle, it could be used to lance a festered sore or operate on lump jaw. Around the camp, it was used as tableware, for skinning a beef for meals, or in games such as mumbley-peg. Most cowboys were content with a sturdy pocket jack-knife or clasp-knife because these models were small and not cumbersome.

Abbott was one cowboy who carried a jack-knife at an early age. He related an incident when he was twelve years of age in which he and his brother had a knife fight because his brother rode one of Abbott's horses without permission:

I thought I was a cowpuncher, and it's a deadly insult to a cowpuncher to ride one of his horses without his permission. We got out our jackknives and flew at each other like a pair of little tigers....[47]

The Barlow knife was popular with the cowboy.[48] A three-bladed pocket model, it was small enough to be carried in a vest or trouser pocket. Some cowboys carried a sheath knife. Like those carried by so many other frontiersmen, this was usually an ordinary butcher knife, such as the famous Green River knife. The sheath was plain leather, sometimes decorated with tacks or bead work.

← Cowboys branding with an early "squeeze chute" near Newcastle, Wyoming, on the Kilpatrick Brothers and Collins home ranch in the late 1890s. Charles Howell is in the center front. Note the two Native American cowboys. *[Anna Miller Museum, Newcastle, Wyoming]*

H O R S E GEAR

← William H. McCabe, a Hulett, Wyoming, cowboy in the early 1920s. Saddles with square skirts and high cantles were still popular among working cowboys on the plains. *[Mrs. Sally Ann Neiman Collection, Hulett, Wyoming]*

Saddles, bridles, bits, cinches, saddle blankets, and the rest of the cowboy's horse equipment have undergone numerous changes in design since the days of the early colonial Spanish settlements in what became the United States. Our research focuses on the Northern Plains area, but several good books listed in this book's bibliography provide a more general study.

Horse equipment was a major investment for a cowboy and, while designs changed throughout the 1800s and 1900s, cowboys were not quick to adopt them. An old saddle was sometimes more valued than a new one. Pre-1890 saddlemaker catalogs are rare but give an accurate picture of who was producing each design during a certain time period. Montgomery Ward catalogs also illustrate horse equipment, although their products reflect designs that sold well over a broad geographic area. The working cowboy in the Northern Plains seldom purchased equipment from general merchandise mail order companies. He preferred instead to buy from local saddle shops or

↳ A variety of leather products were produced by F.A. Meanea in Cheyenne.
[Joseph Palen collection, Cheyenne, Wyoming]

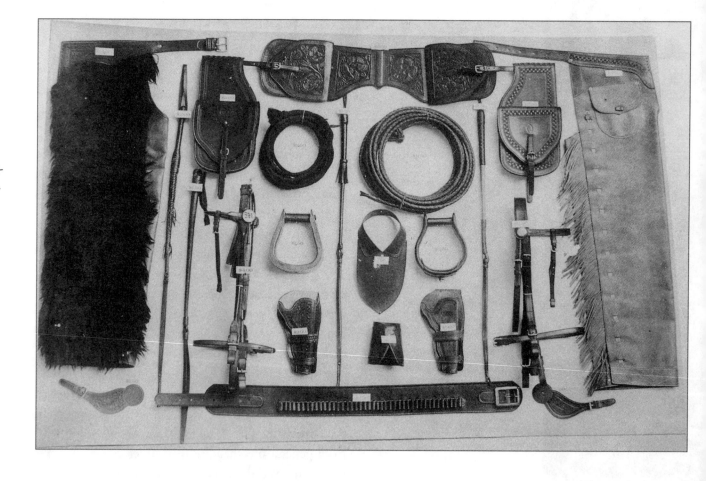

from saddlemaker catalogs because he could trust the quality. Reputable saddlemaking firms used the best leather, saddle trees and craftsmanship and were willing to make custom adaptations, whereas general mercantile stores and catalogs sold items produced uniformly, less expensively, and with varying levels of quality.

The cowboy's horse equipment, much like his personal gear, was predominantly utilitarian. From the bit to the cinch, his primary concern was for the horse, though a little style was thrown into each item.

>─•──○──•──<

SADDLES There was no generic cowboy saddle. The country was too large and the needs of individual regions were too varied to allow such a saddle to evolve. Instead, over the years, regional saddlemakers recognized the needs of their customers and incorporated special designs into their wares accordingly. Many early-model saddles were still produced and used long after they were originally introduced.

Saddles can be grouped according to the position and number of cinches used in rigging the saddle. Single-rigged saddles have one cinch; double-rigged saddles have two. The position of the cinches and cinch rings further identifies the saddle.

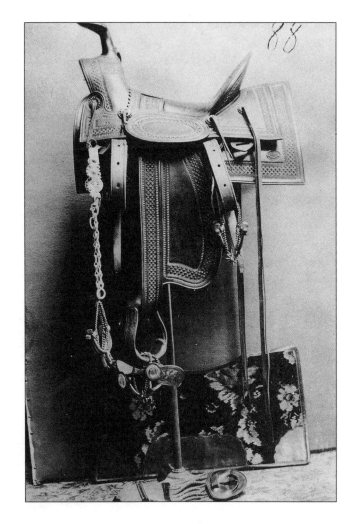

↖ This catalog photograph shows a Donaldson-made saddle, spurs, bit, cinches and corona from about 1900. *[Joseph Palen collection, Cheyenne, Wyoming]*

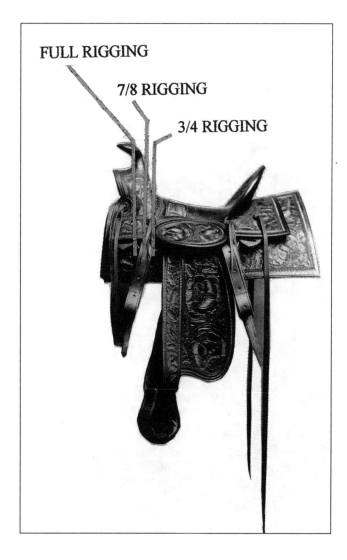

FULL RIGGING

7/8 RIGGING

3/4 RIGGING

→ This illustration labels the various locations for front cinches. This saddle also shows a flank cinch.

Cowboys used three basic styles of double-rigged saddles during the late 1800s. Historic saddle catalogs refer to them as full double-rigged, ⅞-double-rigged, and ¾-double-rigged. The front cinch ring on the full double-rigged saddle was centered below the saddle horn, while it was located 1½ inch to 2 inches further back on the ⅞-rigged saddle. On the ¾-double-rigged saddle the front cinch ring was still further toward the back, approximately three to four inches from a line centered on the saddle horn.

Wyoming and Colorado cowboys of the late nineteenth century generally rode ¾-double-rigged, square skirted saddles. Oregon and California cowboys of the same period typically used single-rigged saddles, while Texans preferred double-rigged models.[1]

The American stock saddle's origin can be traced to the late eighteenth century in Mexico and that portion of southern North America that would become Texas, New Mexico, Arizona and California. This common saddle, in use from Santa Fe to California, was a descendant of the colonial Mexican saddle, called the Spanish-Mexican saddle. Its tree was made of native wood covered with rawhide and then shrouded with a leather covering called a mochila.

← Although this photograph is unidentified and undated, the clarity of the image is remarkable. The man is mounted on what appears to be a Meanea-built single-rigged saddle with a quirt hanging from the saddle horn. It is interesting that the horse wears a snaffle bit. *[Wyoming State Museum]*

↑ Unidentified Fort Bridger, Wyoming, area cowboy in 1884. The man seems to have used this photograph to show his horse and saddle to his friend Hugh Cook. The saddle appears to have been made by J. S. Collins. *[Wyoming State Museum]*

The mochila was removable and frequently had large pockets on each side of the pommel. These early saddles had low sloped cantles, and the early horns had thin necks and relatively small horn caps. While saddle horns first appeared in the mid-1830s, it was not until the late 1840s that they became common. The large dinner-plate horn appeared during the 1860s and was a Mexican innovation that never had much acceptance in the United States.[2] Early Spanish-Mexican saddles had Spanish rigging, in which the single cinch ring was located below and in line with the saddle fork.

The Hope saddle was next in the evolutionary chain. This saddle is sometimes mistakenly called the early Spanish-Mexican saddle. It appeared in Texas around 1846 and was not much more than a rawhide covered tree with a horn and stirrup leathers. Like its progenitor, it had Spanish rigging.

Also appearing in the same time period as the Hope saddle was the California saddle. It had a light-weight, rawhide covered tree encompassed by a mochila, a short-necked horn, a stubby horn cap, no skirts or fenders, and a single-rigging. The predominant rigging pattern in California began with the

↱ Although saddle nomenclature varied some from region to region, these terms were widely used. *[Wyoming State Museum]*

Spanish rigging, but was later replaced with centerfire rigging. These saddles had the rigging ring centered below the middle of the seat. The centerfire saddle was intended for use in flat country and was not designed for heavy roping. It incorporated a wide cinch and was best used on horses with good withers.[3]

By the 1860s a new style of saddle began to appear called the Mother Hubbard. It had a permanently fixed mochila with square corners, no skirts underneath the side bars, cantles generally of medium slope and centerfire rigging. This style did not have fenders on the stirrup leathers; these were not adopted until later years. By 1866, the Mother Hubbard saddle was the one preferred by Texas cowboys on the long trail drives.

Saddle skirts as we know them first appeared in the late 1860s.[4] In the 1870s, saddles began to appear on the western frontiers that utilized both skirts and other design evolutions. California saddles, for example, developed a slightly swelled fork with a high steel horn, steep-pitch six-inch cantles and rounded skirts. The horn had a pitched back cap, ideally suited for the cowboy who dallied his rope. This fork and cantle combination produced a deep seat, well-suited for

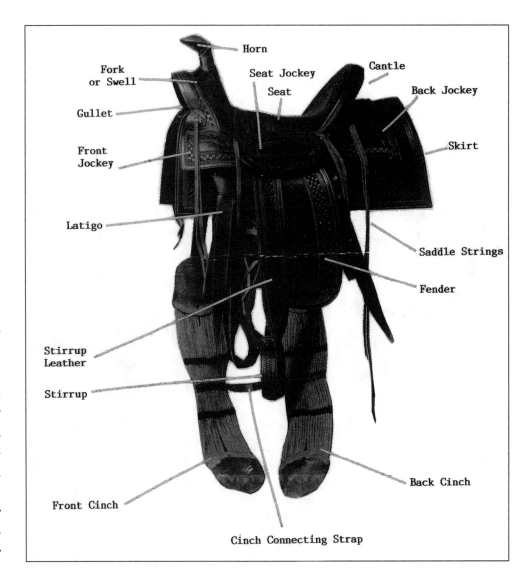

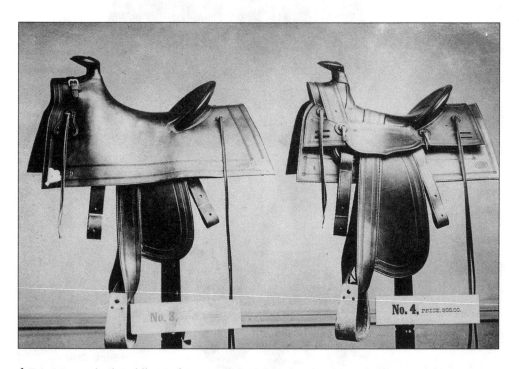

↑ F.A. Meanea built saddles. Left is a Mother Hubbard and right is a half seat with Stagg rigging. *[Joseph Palen collection, Cheyenne, Wyoming]*

use on an unpredictable horse. The rigging, commonly centerfire, was nailed to the tree under the fork cover. Though these saddles were used in Wyoming and Montana, three-quarter double-rigged models were preferred by the cowboys on these ranges, and the skirts were most commonly square instead of rounded. Skirts of the 1870s were lined with wool cloth to help hold the saddle blanket in place. Saddles with sheepskin linings did not appear until 1881.

The loop seat was another innovation of 1870s saddle design, involving an extended seat cover with squares removed to expose the tops of the stirrup leathers as they passed over the tree. This modification allowed access to the stiff stirrup leathers for replacement and cleaning. While records indicate that this seat was developed in the mid-1870s, it did not become popular until around 1885.[5]

Another development of the 1870s was the so-called Sam Stagg rigging. This type of construction affected the front rigging of the saddle. The rigging leather was looped around the horn and went down each side of the slick fork to a rigging ring. Though generally made of one piece of leather, the Sam Stagg

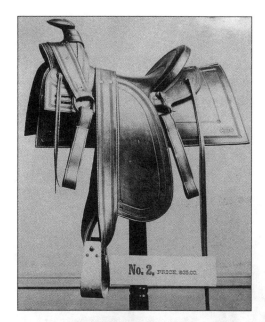

rigging came in various styles. A typical design consisted of two rigging leathers: one passed from the rigging ring up and over the front of the fork of the saddle in front of the horn, while the second front rigging leather looped around the horn.[6]

By the 1880s, most saddlemakers were using iron for saddle horns instead of wood. Patents for a variety of metal saddle horns have been applied for since the late 1860s.

Saddles continued to change as the 1870s came to a close. Long, high-hung fenders appeared on stirrup leathers as the mochila became less popular. Back jockeys (behind the cantle) were also developed during this time. On the Mother Hubbard, single-rigging began to be replaced by three-quarter double-rigging. Texas cowboys used both the dally and hard-and-fast methods of securing their ropes to the saddle horn. It is believed though, that the Texans actually developed the hard-and-fast roping technique, therefore they needed a second cinch to prevent the saddle from tilting upward when the roped cow hit the end of the rope. Thus the double-rigged saddle came into use in which one rigging ring was below the saddle fork and the other below the cantle.[7] The Texas style

↖ F. A. Meanea saddle made in Cheyenne, Wyoming, in the 1890s. Note the Stagg rigging and the Cheyenne cantle roll. *[Joseph Palen collection, Cheyenne, Wyoming]*

↙ Two Meanea-built half seat saddles with Stagg rigging. *[Joseph Palen collection, Cheyenne, Wyoming]*

→ J.S. Collins saddle made in Cheyenne, Wyoming, in the 1890s.

saddle of this period generally had a medium sloped cantle. Finally, all of the 1870s saddles, including those with either the California high back cantle or the Texas sloped cantle, had slick forks.

By the mid-1880s other major changes in saddle design became apparent. A rolled cantle, developed by Cheyenne's Frank Meanea and called the Cheyenne roll, became popular in the early 1880s. The seat jockey made its appearance on saddles in 1885, thus requiring a shorter leather stirrup fender.

Quilted and padded seats date to the earliest Spanish-Mexican saddles. Their appearance on western stock saddles, however, dates to the 1880s. Initially, padded seats were incorporated or inlaid in the saddle's seat instead of being sewn on top. Their popularity was not great among cowboys because they would not dry rapidly after a rain, and a soggy seat was very uncomfortable.[8]

By 1883, the cowboy was becoming a well-known figure in western lore, and mail order catalogs began to reflect this fact. It was in this era that equipment and clothing were first identified as "cowboy." In the 1883 Montgomery Ward summer catalog, the stock saddle first appeared. It was called the "Wyoming

Cow Boy Saddle" and weighed thirty-three pounds. It had a full square skirt, an A-fork pommel and a Cheyenne rolled cantle. It also featured border stamping on the leather and stirrups known as roundhouse or doghouse. The price was $32.20 or, with tapaderos, $36.60. In the same catalog, another stock saddle was offered with fancy flowered tooling. This saddle weighed twenty-eight pounds and cost $28.75 single-rigged with another $1.50 added onto the price if a double rigging was desired.[9]

There were many saddlemakers in the high plains area of Wyoming: E. L. Gallatin, F. A. Meanea, J. S. Collins, Frank Olzer and others. And while these were not the only saddlemakers available to the Wyoming cowboy, they are representative of those who produced saddles at this time. A good saddle by these makers cost the cowboy from forty to one hundred dollars, a substantial investment on cowboy's wages.

Potential customers didn't have to travel to the saddlemaker's shop to buy his wares. Floyd Bard remembered the time he bought a new saddle from a hardware store:

I remember along, in the 1890s when I needed a new saddle and didn't have the cash to buy

← J. B. Trickey in 1912 on a ranch near Lander, Wyoming. The skirts of his saddle have slightly rounded corners reflecting the beginning of change in saddle design. *[Fremont County Pioneer Museum]*

↓ Addison A. Spaugh's horse "Old Cotton" photographed in 1884. The saddle appears to have been made by J. S. Collins. *[Wyoming State Museum]*

one, Mother said to gather in enough fat cattle to buy one. From the range, in among our cattle I gathered in two fat, three-year-old dry heifers, a fat dry cow, and a three-year-old steer, which I sold to the Coslet brothers, Joe and Al, who had a butcher shop in Sheridan. These four head of fat cattle I sold for the sum of sixty dollars (I bought a saddle) at the Otto Kettleson hardware store, where he was selling a saddle that was made by a saddle-maker at Fort Collins, Colorado.

After paying Otto fifty dollars for one of these saddles it didn't leave me much cash, only ten bucks, which nowadays would only buy about what a fellow could put in his vest pocket.[10]

According to O. C. Lapp, a Black Hills cowboy who began his career in 1887,

You could buy from Tom Sweeney hardware or the D. Howe Saddle and Harness shop a crackin' good Cheyenne or Vacilla (sic) tree saddle at from $35 to $40, and I bought Dave's saddle that he had made to order, after he "went west," from Mrs. Clark for $25. He had only used it three seasons.[11]

From the 1880s to the turn of the century, the stock saddle remained relatively unchanged. E. Hough described its value and basic design at the end of the nineteenth century:

> The saddle of the cowboy is the first, last, and most important part of his outfit. It is a curious thing, this saddle developed by the cattle trade, and the world has no other like it. It is not the production of fad, or fancy, but of necessity. Its great weight—a regular cow saddle weighs from thirty to forty pounds...the sturdy frame of a cow saddle will throw the heaviest bull on the range. The saddle is made for riding, upon a country essentially flat. ...The high cantle gives a firmness to the seat of the cowboy when he snubs a steer with a sternness sufficient to send it rolling heels over head. The high pommel, or "horn," steel forged and covered with cross braids of honest leather, serves as anchor post for this same steer, a turn of the rope about it accomplishing that purpose at once.... The long and heavy wooden stirrups seem ungraceful till one has ridden in them, and then he would use no other sort. The strong wooden house of the stirrup protects the foot from being crushed when riding through timber or among cattle or other horses. ...the long cover of leather that sometimes further protects it, neither can the thorns scratch the foot or the limbs of trees drag the foot from its place.[12]

John Rollinson recalled the saddles used on a roundup near Wheatland, Wyoming, in the late 1890s:

> The saddles...were well-built, substantial, plain stock...and mostly bore the name of F. A. Meanea, maker, of Cheyenne. Swelled forks on saddles and fancy show rigging had not come into use at that time, but the horns were low and smaller than formerly, and in this part of the range three-quarter rigs were more popular and in general use, but the double-rig was predominantly the saddle for the older men and the Texas hands that roped a lot.[13]

New innovations—smaller rounded skirts[14] to cut down on weight and swells on the pommel to help the rider stay in the saddle—began to appear after 1900. Low three-inch cantles began appearing on saddles after 1920.[15] Rollinson mentions "a seamless grain sack tied across our saddlebows" that "kept the cold wind out and made a sort of bucking roll" during the fall roundup of 1902 in Goshen Hole.[16] Another item often utilized as a bucking roll was a pommel slicker or a coat. Much later, other changes occurred which were not necessarily visible. For example, because of the increased popularity of the

→ Some popular types of late nineteenth and early twentieth century stirrups. Left to right: Visalia, wide ox-bow, Moran and narrow ox-bow. *[D.E. Walker 1900 catalog. Joseph Palen collection, Cheyenne, Wyoming]*

quarter horse, the bars of the saddle tree were widened to fit this "modern" horse.

⟶·+◦·◦·+◦·◦·+·◦·⟵

STIRRUPS Solid carved wood and iron ring stirrups are the earliest type known to have been used in the American West during the early 1800s. However, it is doubtful that any of these stirrups were used by Wyoming cowmen.

Steamed bent-wood stirrups are known to have existed in the 1860s and maybe earlier. The original bent-wood stirrup was called box, boxcar, or roundhouse because of its large square shape.[17] The first box stirrup had a wide tread, up to eight inches, but as the years passed, saddlemakers experimented with narrowing the sides. Later saddlemakers began covering the outside of wooden stirrups with galvanized iron, eventually changing to brass. The next improvement was to cover the tread with leather in order to decrease wear. Finally, the whole wooden stirrup was encased with leather or rawhide. Addison Spaugh, a cowboy who came to Wyoming in the 1870s, preferred roundhouse stirrups on his J.S. Collins saddle, made during the first half of the 1880s.[18]

The ox-bow was a narrow, round-bottomed stirrup which derived its name from its similarity to an ox yoke's bow. Ox-bow stirrups began replacing the box style toward the end of the 1880s. They allowed the rider to place his foot in the stirrup all the way to the heel of his boot, thus allowing the boot heel to lock into the stirrup. The old-time cowboys claimed this made for both a more secure stirrup when on a bucking horse and for a far less fatiguing ride.

Catalogs from the late nineteenth and early twentieth centuries generally offered many different types of stirrups. Some had springs and others had a ninety-degree swivel which allowed them to hang straight without twisting the stirrup leathers.[19] While innovative stirrups were continually being introduced, such as the hand-forged iron, the Moran, and the Visalia patterns,[20] such changes were resisted by the cowboy. Virtually every historic photograph, along with original saddles in museum collections, shows the more standard styles of stirrups. Ramon Adams described the most common types of stirrups:

The old wide wooden stirrups of the early range were called "dog-house stirrups," "ox-bows," or "ox-yokes." With the evolution of the saddle came narrower stirrups which made it easier to mount and dismount.... The Visalia style was a fav'rite, and was wide 'nough to let a man put his weight on the ball of his foot. It had flarin' sides and a flat bottom. The bronc stirrup has a narrow bottom, as most riders like to have

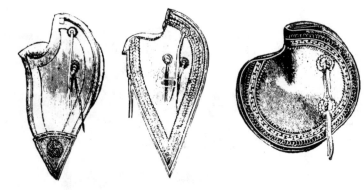

their feet well in the stirrups, but can easily kick their feet free.[21]

Although rarely used today, the tapadero was once a popular component of the stirrup. A fad among Wyoming cowboys, the tapadero was originally designed to protect the rider's foot from brush. It also provided protection from the cold winds. Basically two types of tapaderos, sometimes called taps, were commonly used. The bulldog or monkey nose was so called because of their resemblance to those animals' heads. The eagle bill was a showier tap with a long flowing appearance. It could also be used by a skilled horseman in turning a cow by popping the long leather tips against the animal.[22]

⌐ Tapaderos as illustrated in the D. E. Walker 1900 catalog. Left to right: Visalia style eagle bill, eagle bill and bull or monkey nosed taps. *[Joseph Palen collection, Cheyenne, Wyoming]*

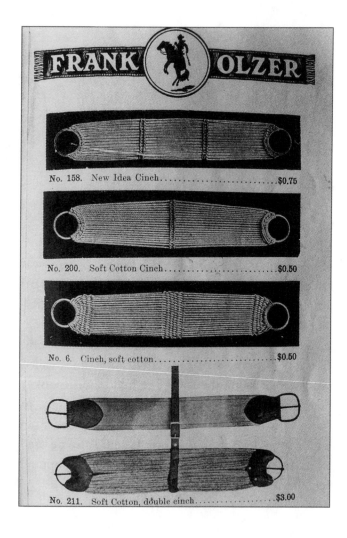

→ Types of cinches offered by Frank Olzer in his 1905 catalog. *[Joseph Palen collection, Cheyenne, Wyoming]*

Tapaderos had other purposes in working with stock. Steve Nevil, for example, used them to assist in breaking horses:

When the horse would begin to balk, I would reach up with one foot and slap the flap on the horse's head. You had better have honey on your pants when you do this, because they turn real quick. I would slacken the reins and then snap them with the tap.[23]

CINCHES   Often overlooked by researchers, the cinch had as many variants as any other piece of horse gear. An 1880s J. S. Collins & Company catalog offered ten different types of cinches.[24] While the majority of them were hair cinches, the type of hair was of the buyer's choosing. Examples included sixteen-strand buffalo hair, eighteen-strand Angora goat hair, thirty-strand white horse hair, and white cotton strand. Because they were sturdy and economical, the cotton and fish cord cinches seem to have been the most common varieties used for both front and flank cinches during the 1870s and 1880s.

By the 1890s, cotton web cinches were offered in saddlemaker catalogs. These were intended for use as flank cinches on double-rigged saddles. Near the end of the nineteenth century, leather flank cinches appeared, similar to those sold today.[25]

Regardless of the cinch's composition, the rings were normally leather bound with the buckle ring as common as the plain ring. A quick release device, called a tackaberry, was introduced around 1900.

>─◆─○─◇─<

SADDLEBAGS   While not essential or often used, saddlebags, also known as saddle pockets or Cheyenne pockets, were a desirable addition to any cowboy's horse equipment. Research indicates that working cowboys generally did not use saddlebags. However, if a cowboy was riding line or doing some other chore which required him to be riding alone, pockets did come in handy. During the 1902 fall roundup in the Goshen Hole, John Rollinson remarked that the roundup foreman carried his tally book "in his saddle pockets."[26] Generally speaking, though, saddlebags were a luxury that most cowboys could not afford.

In contrast to today's saddlebags, which almost resemble panniers because of their immense size, a turn-of-the-century cowboy's saddle pockets were relatively small. For example, a large pair measured

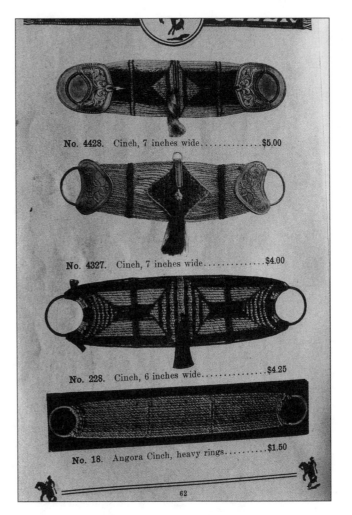

No. 4428.   Cinch, 7 inches wide.............$5.00

No. 4327.   Cinch, 7 inches wide.............$4.00

No. 228.   Cinch, 6 inches wide.............$4.25

No. 18.   Angora Cinch, heavy rings.........$1.50

62

← Several types of cinches were offered by Frank Olzer in his 1905 catalog. *[Joseph Palen collection, Cheyenne, Wyoming]*

approximately eight inches high, eight inches wide and three inches deep.[27]

Custom saddles could have saddlebags permanently affixed. It was also common to have angora, buffalo or bear pocket flaps.[28] Most likely these fur coverings were a fad and served no practical function. The contention that fur coverings shed water is incorrect as the fur actually tended to catch moisture instead of shedding it.

The U.S. Army was a cheap source for saddlebags. Army saddlebags were an inexpensive addition and, like so many other military surplus items, were generally a good value for the money. If possible, cowboys purchased or swapped these items from soldiers.

The staple pocket originated in the 1860s as an ammunition pouch. As fences became common, the pouches were used to carry fence repair staples.[29] R. T. Frazier offered a staple pocket in his 1907 catalog which could be tied to a saddle by the saddle strings.

Another item rarely used was the cantena. This was a saddle pocket that fit over the saddle horn and draped over the pommel. These small leather pouches closely resembled the Cheyenne pocket in size and shape.

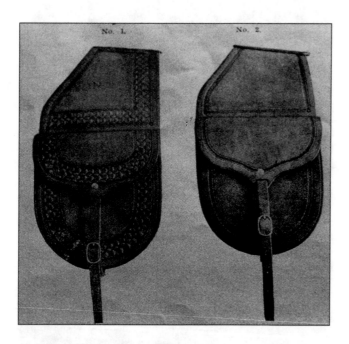

↳ Common style saddle pockets made by R. T. Frazier, Pueblo, Colorado. *[Joseph Palen collection, Cheyenne, Wyoming]*

SADDLE BLANKETS During the heyday of
the Wyoming cowboy, the choice of saddle blanket
was a matter of individual preference. There were
many different options open to the cowboy wanting
to protect his horse from the chafing caused by
heavy saddles.

The performance of the saddle blanket depended
on it being properly folded, and care had to be taken
to prevent wrinkles, twigs or dirt from becoming
trapped beneath the saddle causing rubbing and cre-
ating tender sores on the horse's back. Blankets
which dried quickly were preferred. If the cowboy
anticipated heavy riding, he used a combination of
saddle blankets and pads to provide extra protection.

A wool Army blanket[30] was hard to beat, particularly if a square piece of burlap was placed under the
blanket for extra ventilation.[31] The burlap soaked the
sweat from the back of the horse while the large holes
in the fabric allowed a consistent flow of air to cool
the animal's back.

Other options included the Navajo blanket, the
felt pad, the corona, and the hair pad.[32] All of these
blankets and pads had been available since the early
1870s, but the Navajo blanket was the most desired.

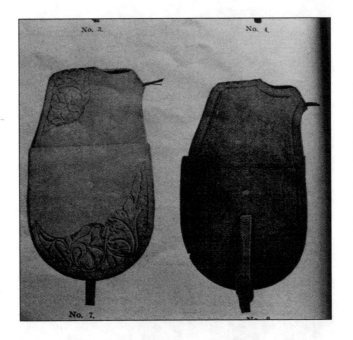

↑ Cantenas were made to hang from the saddle horn, whereas
saddle bags were attached behind the cantle. These cantenas
were made by R.T. Frazier,. *[Joseph Palen collection, Cheyenne,
Wyoming]*

↑ Fence staple pocket. *[R.T.
Frazier 1907 catalog. Joseph
Palen collection, Cheyenne,
Wyoming]*

→ Near Photo: Typical Navajo saddle blankets as illustrated in the Otto F. Ernest catalog. *[Joseph Palen collection, Cheyenne, Wyoming]*

→ Far Photo: Three common saddle pads available before 1900. *[Frank Olzer catalog, Joseph Palen collection, Cheyenne, Wyoming]*

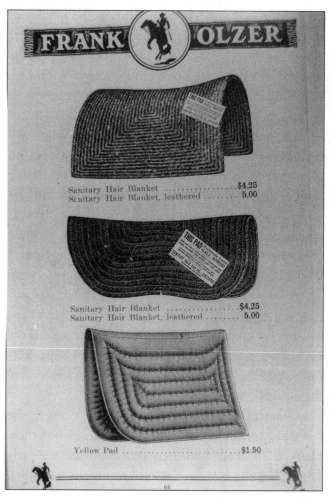

In his book *Pulling Leather,* author Reuben B. Mullins states: "Cowpunchers found that the Indian Blankets were the best saddle blankets they could find, and the boys were always on the lookout for them."[33] Indian blankets were generally produced by the Navajos. They came in various geometric designs or striped patterns and sometimes employed both motifs.

Navajo saddle blankets were made of heavy woven wool, were sold by the pound, and came in two sizes. The single size measured 17 inches by 32 inches and weighed between two-and-one-half and four pounds, while double weight blankets ranged between five and ten pounds and were normally 64 inches by 34 inches.

The corona is not as well known as other saddle protection. This shaped pad was designed to be used in lieu of or over a blanket and was generally leather trimmed.[34] Coronas were quite well liked but their high cost was prohibitive for most cowboys, hence their lack of widespread usage.

Felt saddle blankets (called pads) were covered with duck, lined with felt and stuffed with hair. These pads were quilted to keep the filling in place. The duck coverings were available in a variety of colors,

↑ The Laramie Kid near Cheyenne, Wyoming in the 1890s. A braided hair saddle pad can be seen beneath the saddle skirts. *[Wyoming State Museum]*

→ In this Donaldson Saddlery illustration a floral corona is shown accompanying the saddle. *[Joseph Palen collection, Cheyenne, Wyoming]*

but were predominately yellow, red and blue. In 1898, a felt-less saddle pad was developed with soft, flexible stuffing guaranteed not to mat or knot.[35]

One of the most popular saddle blankets was the King's Pure Hair blanket. It was made of woven animal hair and had a cloth binding along the bottom edges. It was popular because it allowed maximum air circulation and easily conformed to the horse's back. Unfortunately, these early pads were known to carry anthrax spores and their use was soon discontinued.[36]

Another saddle pad commonly seen in historic catalogs is the Sanitary Hair Pad Company's hair blanket. It utilized curled hair and was covered in cloth.

BREAST COLLARS & HALTERS Two items of horse equipment which are virtually never referenced are the halter and the breast collar. This is probably because, according to vintage photographs and contemporary accounts between 1880 and 1920, they were rarely used by the average cowboy. Historic accounts indicate that starting about 1930, trick riders were the first non-military users of breast collars. Halters are rarely if ever seen in photographs of cowboys and no historic accounts indicate their use either. They were only used in stables or when horses were placed on a picket line.

◄►•◦•◄►

BRIDLES & BITS The bridle usually has four components: the headstall, bit, curb strap and reins. With the exception of the bit, this piece of horse gear has probably resisted change more than any other item of cowboy equipment. There were variations of course: some headstalls had a brow band which connected the cheek pieces over the forehead, while others had an ear loop which slipped over one or two of the horse's ears. Most bridles also had a throat latch which connected the bridle under the horse's jaw, securing the bridle to the head.

Leather and rawhide headstalls were popular with the working cowboy because of their strength. Those made of leather were often wide, tooled affairs decorated with metal conchas.[37] Narrow plain leather headstalls were also used and generally had few if any conchos. Rawhide headstalls were usually simple in design, with the finer braided types considered works of art today. Braided horse hair headstalls seem to have been used primarily for show or other dress up occasions but were rarely used while working.

↑ This photograph of a night hawk was taken near Cheyenne, Wyoming, in the late 1890s. Note that he is using a corona and a single rigged saddle. *[Wyoming State Museum]*

Through examination of historic documents, catalogs and photographs, the curb bit appears to be the most common type used with bridles during the late nineteenth and early twentieth centuries. As with most bits, the curb bit consisted of several parts: the mouth piece with different sized ports, the side bars, and sometimes a tie bar joining the side bars near where the reins were attached. It was available with low, high or medium ports. In the wrong hands, the higher ports could create pain when worked in the horse's mouth, but when used properly they were not considered severe.

The spade bit had a definite Spanish influence, using a deep port, spoon, and cricket, or other hardware attached to the port.[38] These bits were generally quite ornamental with silver inlays and conchas.

The half-breed bit was also popular. Incorporating the best of the curb and spade bits, it normally had a high port with a cricket and ornate cheek pieces.[39]

Bits and spurs were often made by local blacksmiths for both individual stockmen and saddlemakers. Floyd Bard recalled that some cowboys had bridle bits that had been "made by one of the Merrill boys, who was a blacksmith."[40] Meanea Saddlery in Cheyenne, contracted for bridle bits with Holden Peterson, a blacksmith in the late 1880s from the town of Fort Fetterman, Wyoming. It seems that Mr. Peterson was behind on production as Meanea wrote:

...I am laying in a heavy stock & need all the cash can get holt of & you wont even explain why you do not send the $150.00 which promised to send as soon as got to Fetterman. Straighten out. I do not consider you are acting the part of an honest man, & unless you answer this in a reasonable length of time you will hear from me & dont forget it. I want my money or some Bits, & you can at least write me or have some one do so for you explaining what you will do or can do regarding the matter.[41]

John B. Kendrick also ordered a bridle bit from Peterson. The blacksmith was able to produce for Kendrick, as Peterson wrote on July 12, 1889:

Your letter of July 2nd com to my hand tow days ago at Inez where I have been to work the last month. I got home at noon day befor yesterday, and have been to work on you Bitt as hard as I could, But got to late about 15 minuts to git it on the Stage tonight. I do not know if I will git it on the train tomorow or not. If it comes to late please send it bak to me.[42]

↓ This Frank Meanea catalog illustration shows his selection of bits, spurs, rosets, bit chains and steel saddle horns. *[Joseph Palen collection, Cheyenne, Wyoming]*

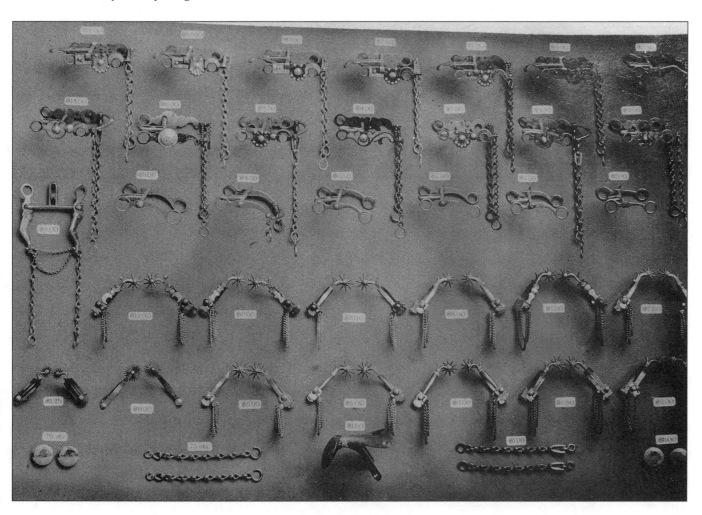

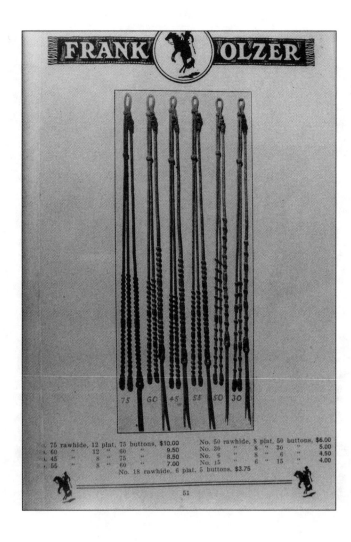

→ This illustration from a 1905 Frank Olzer catalog shows rawhide closed reins. *[Joseph Palen collection, Cheyenne, Wyoming]*

Seldom seen in western lore or movies, but quite a significant piece of horse equipment during the nineteenth and twentieth centuries, was the hackamore. The hackamore consisted of a crown, plain leather cheek straps and a noseband or bosal frequently made of braided rawhide.[43] John Barrows told of breaking cow-horses using a hackamore:

> At all events, half strangled, snorting, trembling and enraged, he was first subjected to the indignity of a jaquima, or "hackamore." This was a very effective braided rawhide halter, with a hard rounded noseband . . .[44]

Hackamores were also made from hemp or rope. They could be purchased from saddle shops, but were often made by cowboys or even convicted criminals serving prison sentences.

Mecate ropes were part of the hackamore, serving as lead ropes and reins. They also were used to help train the horse in reining.

Some cowboys used a mecate separately from the hackamore as a lead rope. Photographs have been found showing its use in this manner. In these images the mecate is shown coiled and tied to the saddle. It then extends from the saddle and is tied around the horse's neck. In 1903, Rollinson states that until he rode for a horse wrangling crew near Thermopolis, Wyoming, he:

> ...never knew anything of men riding for horse outfits who rode with the looped-up end of the mecate (the hemp or hair rope that runs down from the hackamore bossel which is ordinary tied on the left side of the saddlebow by the short saddle string). We had two men who were from eastern Oregon—one from the John Day country and the other from the Wallowa Mountain Country.... These two horsemen always tucked the coiled-up loop of the mecate into their waistband, under their cartridge belt or chaps belt. The idea was a good one for running horses in a rough country, for if one's horse falls, the rider has a chance to grab that fourteen or sixteen-foot line and keep from getting set afoot, with miles between himself and camp. The idea was readily adopted by all riders on that range in those days, I too followed this precautionary custom and it twice saved me from being set afoot....[45]

Reins were the final component of the bridle and these too came in many different styles. In the 1913 Hamley and Company catalog, reins were offered in leather of varying widths, from five-eighths to one inch. The common length averaged seven feet and all included a romal, or quirt end. The 1921 White and Davis catalog offered reins in either skirting or latigo leather, with the same widths as the Hamley catalog. Reins were not solely made of solid leather: many were produced using braided rawhide.

Bit chains, commonly called rein chains, were light metal chains about one foot in length. The ends of the reins attached to the rings on the bit chain and the chains in turn were linked to the bit. These were sometimes called slobber chains, but this was merely a form of slang. Their functional purpose was two-fold: they acted as a shock-absorbing unit and as an extension of the bit, serving to balance it. When the bit rested in the horse's mouth and the reins were slack in the rider's hands, the weight of the chains caused them to fold downward between the bit rings and the reins. When the reins were drawn tight, the chains (by slowly straightening), eased the motion on the bit in the horse's mouth. A properly balanced bit aided in the comfort of the horse, and bit chains added this balance on heavier bits.[46]

Reins were offered in two general types: closed and open. Cowboys from Texas or those with a strong

⌐ Various styles of bit reins with romals attached as illustrated in the D.E. Walker, Visalia Stock Saddle Company catalog, 1900. *[Reprinted by permission of Zon International Publishing.]*

VISALIA STOCK SADDLE CO. 43

MEXICAN REINS.

No. 5.
4 plait, $2.00.

No. 7.
4 plait 16 buttons,
$2.75.

No. 9.
6 plait, 15 buttons, $3.50.

No. 11.
8 plait, 54 buttons, $4.50.

No. 13.
Extra fine, 12 plait buttons, $6.00.

No. 30.
Flat black leather, $1.25.

These rawhide reins are all handmade by the best Mexican rein maker in the State, who also makes our reatas, quirts, and all our rawhide work. Our No. 11 has 54 buttons on the reins and romal, and is the best rein in the market for the price. Try a pair, and if not satisfactory we will return money and take them back.

No. 32.
Round, with nickel ring, $3.00.

Texas influence generally favored open reins. West coast cowboys from California, Oregon and Washington were partial to closed reins. Most of the saddlemaker's catalogs illustrated the closed rein variety, but all carried open reins as well.

Open reins were not joined together at the saddle-end. This made it less likely that a grazing horse would get its reins caught in the brush, allowing the cowboy to train his mount to be ground tied. Either one or both reins were dropped on the ground, so that if the horse tried to get away, it would step on one of the reins and stop itself.[47] Ground tying was necessary on the open plains as there were few trees and bushes where the cowboy could tie his horse.

Closed reins were connected at the saddle-end and usually had a romal extending past the connected ends. In other ways, they were made like open reins.

━━◆━○━◆━━

Cowboys took pride in owning respected horse gear. Respect was earned by gear which was rugged, utilitarian, and fairly priced. However, appearance and style sometimes also played a role in what a cowboy selected.

⌐ "T" Ranch cowboys rope remounts during the 1886 roundup on the Cheyenne River in Wyoming. William J. Cool is the cowboy in the center. *[Wyoming State Museum]*

CHAPTER FIVE

BEDROLLS, CAMP EQUIPMENT & CHUCK WAGONS

BEDROLLS The cowboy's bedroll originally began with just blankets, heavy quilts, or comforters called soogans. Most cowboys could not afford to purchase a piece of canvas or tarpaulin to use as an outside wrapping. John Rollinson stated that his first bedroll in 1902 was merely "woolen blankets and a sugan or two." [1] Such wrappings were not always necessary in the southwest, but on the colder and wetter northern plains, tarpaulins, called tarps, were needed to repel rain and snow. John B. Kendrick explained in a letter to a friend:

> My introduction to the use or merits of a tarpaulin came coincidentally with your own. While on my original trip over the Texas trail I bunked with the same Sam Moses referred to in your letter and I recall distinctly that our bed included one pair of blankets owned by him and two that I owned, an inequality against me on account of the disproportion of capital invested in the bed used between us.

← Unidentified chuck wagon in the Cheyenne, Wyoming, area during the late 1890s. *[Wyoming State Museum]*

↑ Chuck wagon filled with bedrolls at mouth of Horse Creek near Cheyenne, Wyoming, in 1885. *[American Heritage Center]*

The tarpaulin referred to in the stampede of the remuda, was no doubt one that I used on my second trip over the trail during the Spring and Summer of 1884, five years after the original trip. As it happened I was in charge of this herd myself, and because of the demoralization toward extravagance occasioned by three or four years on the Northern range the men, including myself, not only had tarpaulins for their beds but we had a good many things to eat that were not in evidence during the first trip.[2]

Teddy Blue Abbott recalled that the bedrolls of the 1870s were simple and limited:

Lay on your saddle blanket and cover up with a coat was about the only bed used on the Texas trail at first. A few had a big buffalo robe to roll up in, but if they ever got good and wet you never had time to dry them, so they were not popular.[3]

Bob Fudge, another Texas cowboy who moved also to Wyoming, said that in 1882 his first bedroll was a very basic one which did not have "a rainproof tarpaulin." He said that he was "allowed to take as bedding a couple of blankets" on his first trail drive from Texas.[4]

↓ Dinner at a roundup camp near Cheyenne, Wyoming. This photo was taken in 1898 by Joseph Stimson. Captions and commentary were provided in 1921 by Ashley Gleason, roundup foreman in the photograph. Left to right: "William Fry, photographer, northern New Mexico; L.T. Bennett, busily engaged in cutting a tough beefsteak, Fort Duckane [Duchesne], Utah; Perry Williams, Cheyenne; Charles Phelps, Casper [partially hidden by Williams]; Lon Roach, now state law enforcement official [later 1934 warden of state penitentiary]; Roy Baxter, government pack master; Bob Van Horn, son of commanding officer at Fort Russell; Dick Dummet, A.P.O. rep; [this man] was such a poor rep was sent home with his string, and gladly were the neck tie horses gathered for him; Pete Anderson, didn't want to hide his face with a cup, but his eagerness to get the sugar settlings, was caught in the act. Pete was as good a day jingler as any, even though he was a Swede. He was a physical wreck following the Spanish-American War; Joe Benjamine wanted to be sure of getting in, so took to the top of the mess box; Guy McNurlen, a wonderful buster, he has fought many a wild bronk at Frontier Days; Bill Hosack, Granite Canyon, Wyo., he is wearing among the first angora schaps introduced into this country; Ed Clark, Virginia Dale, Wyo [Colorado]; Joe Detrick, has probably attained greater wealth than any one of the bunch. He left riding because he couldn't stick with them. He began mining and later accumulated much wealth; Ashley L. Gleason, in 1921 was foreman for the Fiddleback Co., wool growers Douglas, Wyo; George Johnson, now in California." [Wyoming State Museum]

↓ Roundup crew on Prairie Dog Creek, about 1885.
[American Heritage Center]

By the mid 1880s, most cowboys seem to have tarpaulins to cover their bedrolls. This is evident in the historic photographs. Harry Williams, a cowboy from Big Horn, Wyoming, said that winter bedrolls cost about $100 and that:

> Blankets could be purchased at this time in the Big Horn Basin varying, in weight from 2 ½ lbs. to 20 lbs each. If a cowhand possessed a bed roll consisting of two of these 20 lb. blankets and a tarpaulin, he could sleep on ice and yet be warm, simply by doubling the width of the blankets for they were very wide. A good tarp was a necessity of course. The complete winter bed weight between 75 and 100 lbs. Many cannot understand how the cowboy survived the terrible winters when even the cattle perished. The answer was his bed roll.[5]

According to Ben Bird and Sam Hotchkiss, these tarpaulins were "about eighteen feet long and six feet wide, that was doubled over from the bottom up and tucked under the sleeper on each side."[6]

Shy Ousterhout recalled "that a few tarps were seen with a series of rings and snaps sewn on the sides, to help keep the bedroll together."[7] In his reminiscences, Harry Williams remarked that one cowboy

↖ The T 7 outfit eating dinner during the 1895 roundup near Gillette, Wyoming. The cook was Alex Mashek. *[Wyoming State Museum]*

named Captain Belmont had his "tarpaulin sewed up the sides."[8]

Other than soogans, army and Navajo blankets were popular, as was the California blanket, a finely woven wool cloth with a hard smooth surface that shed both water and soil.[9] A cheap, light weight, feather-filled comforter or simple blanket called a henskin was employed by the less fortunate cowboy.[10]

Due to the size of these rolls, any cowboy traveling or going to a roundup had his bedroll strapped to a pack horse. While on a roundup, bedrolls were most often carried in the bed wagon. However, the poorer ranch outfits at times did not have bed wagons, and thus the rolls were carried by pack animals or on the chuck wagon.

WARBAGS The warbag was the cowboy's valise or suitcase. It was made of cotton or canvas and varied in size depending upon what the cowboy could afford or find. Most warbags were merely a two-bushel seamless cotton grain sack, tied shut at the opening by a string or leather thong and containing clothing and personal grooming items. This proved inexpensive and easily replaceable. Harry

→ Carter Cattle Company roundup on Smith's Fork, near Fort Bridger in 1886. The men mounted on horses are James Valdez, Al Heater, George Harvey, Neal Nielson. Bob Hamilton is standing with hands in pockets. *[Wyoming State Museum]*

Schlosher spoke of the contents of a cowboy's warbag: "…something like two suits of underwear, a spare shirt, some socks, and a little loose personal stuff." [11] Rollinson also recalled that the warbag was used for clothing as well as various personal articles:

> One fellow produced a razor, cake of soap, and a towel, together with a small hand mirror, which he hung on the endgate rod of the bed wagon. Another man got out a clean shirt, while a third dug up a sewing outfit — a small leather bag containing thread, needles (in a wooden case), beeswax, and spare buttons of various sorts — and, after selecting two buttons, sewed them where they were most needed on a spare pair of California pants. [12]

If the cowboy was traveling with only his saddle horse, he would, of course, carry less in his warbag. Generally he strapped his bag behind the cantle of the saddle. Floyd Bard remembered, when he became a horse wrangler in the fall of 1889, "…Mother tied my little war bag (sack of clothing) on back of my saddle…." [13] Rollins says, "The war sacks were laid directly upon the pack-saddle, one on each of its sides and one atop it…." [14]

Warbags would also be carried if the cowboy was traveling by stage, wagon or railroad. Bard, traveling by spring wagon to Montana in 1900, recalled, "…all the baggage I had was a war bag with my clothes and my cowboy outfit in a gunny sack." [15]

↙ This 1880s photograph shows a typical arrangement of cooking utensils in a chuck wagon. Nate Champion (third from right) was killed in the Johnson County War in 1892. Dudley Champion is on the far right. [*Wyoming State Museum*]

↑ The Studebaker "Roundup Wagon" as illustrated in the Studebaker Brothers Manufacturing Company catalog of 1887. [*Berkebile*, Horse-Drawn Commercial Vehicles]

COOKING EQUIPMENT When working the range without a chuck wagon, few cowboys carried any cooking paraphernalia. When forced to make an overnight stay, the cowboy simply killed some wild game and roasted it over an open fire, or went without eating until he arrived at another camp or found a homestead. However, if he was planning a trip for several days and knew no food could be found, he might carry enough provisions within his blankets or slicker. Rollins states:

> If a cowboy were starting a trip which, while forcing him to camp overnight, did not call for many supplies and a consequent pack-horse, he would, nevertheless, not limit himself to the traditional Hudson Bay Company's ration of rabbit track and cartridge, but would insert within the folds of the "slicker" tied at his saddle's rear the journey's necessaries. These were a frying-pan, some flour, bacon, coffee, salt, and as a substitute for yeast, either a bottle of sour dough or a can of baking-powder.[16]

When traveling alone the cowboy merely did the best he could in finding food and water, and at times endured many a hungry and thirsty journey.

➤⊷⊙⊷◄

↓ Bar C, Studebaker Roundup Wagon, 1884. Standing: Hank Dovoe, Ray Peters, George Gordon, Cheston Morris, Nate Champion, Joe Vincent. Seated: Buck Jackson, unknown, Hall, unknown, unknown, Al Allison, Bill Rankin, Jack Flagg.

Flagg and Champion were major players in the Johnson County War. This wagon is the same brand as the one drawn on the left. *[Wyoming State Museum]*

↰ Cowboys from Addison Spaugh's roundup crew are seated in front of their chuck wagon near the 77 ranch near Lusk, Wyoming. The cowboys are Davis Cook, Bob Hester, Oscar Keithley Guy Shipley, an unidentified man, Charles Bright, Louis Ryan, Burr Shipley, Roy Rogers, and Newt Dupes. *[Wyoming State Museum]*

Chuck Wagons & Bed Wagons

A roundup in Wyoming would not have been complete without the chuck wagon. In fact, a ranch crew was known as belonging to a specific wagon or brand. For example, the cowboys said they "belonged to" the Two Bar wagon or the Rafter Y Bar wagon, and so forth. There were generally several chuck wagons at each individual roundup each representing a particular ranch. They started on the perimeter of the area and moved closer to the gathered herd each day.

Each chuck wagon carried food, cooking equipment and sometimes firewood. After 1890, a cook tent and stove was often added to the cooking equipment. In the rear of each chuck wagon was a cupboard with a door that opened downward. When open, this door served as a food preparation area and serving table for the cook. When closed, the door secured the food and cooking equipment held within.

Few wagon manufacturing firms made chuck boxes for their wagons. The majority were instead

crafted to the individual rancher's specifications either on the ranch or in nearby communities. One firm, Studebaker Brothers Manufacturing Company of South Bend, Indiana, did produce a "Round-Up Wagon" as early as 1887. This wagon was specially designed for the rancher and his needs.[17]

Accompanying the chuck wagon was the bed wagon. While the former carried the food stuffs and cooking equipment, the latter transported the bedrolls, tents, branding irons, corral ropes and other general equipment necessary during the roundup. Another purpose of the bed wagon was to serve as a second anchor for the rope corral which held the cowboys' horses while the cowboys selected their mounts. Every morning the night hawk or horse wrangler brought in the horses. They were herded into a rope corral which terminated with the bed wagon on one corner and the chuck wagon on the other. Heavy ropes were spread out in the general shape of a funnel and held about two feet off the

↳ Chuck wagon and camp of the 101 ranch near Moorcroft, Wyoming, in 1887. John Winterling fore-man, is fourth from left, front row, with striped pants and bandanna. [*American Heritage Center*]

↗ The Trabing Brothers ranch chuck wagon near Chugwater, Wyoming, in the 1880s. *[Wyoming State Museum]*

ground by either the cowboys or small posts. The herd was run into this improvised corral, and the cowboys entered its confines to rope their chosen horse for the morning's work. After the horses were roped and saddled, the day herder took the remaining herd out for grazing until a change of horses was needed by the cowboys.

These two wagons were made by any number of wagon-making firms, but the most prominently used on the Wyoming range seem to have been the Bain Wagon Company and Studebaker Brothers Manufacturing Company. John Rollinson describes the "Bain Wagon" that served as a chuck wagon:

What a marvelously useful work these seventeen men and the cook could accomplish over a rough country of few roads and fewer bridges, with long distances between the settlements, and longer miles to the stores! The two wagons in use were comparatively new, particularly the chuck wagon, which was a Bain wagon. The bed wagon was somewhat lighter, as the chuck wagon hauled the heaviest loads. The mess box, built on the rear end, was well made, and the drawers and compartments well arranged.... Things were kept in order, for the outfit could not long function if the foreman, the cook, and every man did not do his part to maintain order. If a man carelessly lost even a spoon and did not find it and put it in its place, the loss might make some one short before another could be supplied.[18]

John Barrows, who rode for the DHS ranch in Montana, recalled their 1883 roundup chuck wagon:

He drove a fiery team of four outlaw horses, spoiled in the breaking, but willing to perform in harness. His mess wagon was a three-inch Schuttler, with a double box and excellent canvas cover well stretched over the bows. The rear end of this wagon was replaced by a well-built cupboard the exact width of the wagon box and about four feet high. The broad door to this cupboard, hinged at the bottom, could be lowered, discovering the cupboard contents stowed on their shelves, and it served as the cook's table. The forward part of the wagon carried the bulk of our provisions, sacks of flour, sides of bacon, sugar, hominy, rice, and beans, dried apples and peaches in boxes, canned tomatoes in cases (the only canned goods furnished), and perhaps a small supply of potatoes. In order that our commissary department might be self-contained, this wagon carried also the cook tent with its poles and gear.

In moving from corral to corral, or from camp to camp on the trail, Johnny with his outfit and the driver of the bed wagon who hauled with almost similar equipment the bedding, tents, branding irons, and so forth, piloted their caravan over untracked prairie, through unbridged streams, down and up ungraded hills, to destinations sometimes unknown, or indicated in the morning by a pointed finger and two or three words descriptive. At noon we would find Old Johnny fully established and at home, with a satisfying hot meal ready for our unqualified appetites.[19]

Chuck wagons and bed wagons were a necessary part of a roundup and remained in service on many ranches after the advent of the automobile. Eventually the wagon disappeared but the chuck box was placed in the rear of a pick-up truck and continued in service.

THE REAL COWBOY

← These cowboys stopped for dinner during the Indian Creek Roundup. This scene was photographed one mile south of the Hat Creek Store near Lusk, Wyoming, in July 1910. Left to right: George Putman, Dade Bond, Burt Putman, Jack Hiblen, George Hill, Ed White, Jack Hunter, Billy Marking, unknown, Chet Arlington (cook, standing), Jess Boner, unknown, unknown, Eaf Hogg, Bob Woody, Oat Hill, All Ardman, Roy Casady, Nance Ming, unknown, unknown, Art Beam, Lee Yocum and Tom Wilson. *[Wyoming State Museum]*

Now, as it was in earlier times, it is easy to distinguish the real working cowboy from the "drugstore" variety. Although the wool vest has given way to the down vest and the Stetson has succumbed to the "King Ropes" baseball cap, the Wyoming cowboy's demand for utility in work clothing has changed little.

Likewise, horse gear has changed considerably in the past one hundred years: saddles with rounded skirts and swells have replaced the old square skirted, "A" forked saddles and braided nylon reins on aluminum or stainless steel bits have frequently replaced those of leather and iron. Nevertheless, the basis for this equipment—utility of purpose—remains the same.

In searching for the definitive cowboy "uniform," evidence indicates that no such article has ever existed. The cowboy was an individual and was proud of that fact. He was generally conservative and would dress in accordance with his personality or finances.

↵ George Hiteshew drives the chuck wagon for his round-up crew near Manville, Wyoming, in the 1910s. *[Janette Chambers Collection]*

Like everyone else, he bought clothing and gear to suit his own personal needs.

Adaptability has been the key to the survival of both the cowboy's gear and the cowboy himself. If, for example, a given style of saddle worked well for one task but not many tasks, it simply wasn't used. The same could be said for the cowboy. If he had not adapted from open-range ranching to fenced-in ranching, he would have disappeared along with the stagecoach and the pony express.

E N D N O T E S

1. THE NORTHERN PLAINS COWBOY

1. *Cheyenne* (Wyoming) *Daily Leader,* 10 November 1881.

2. *Cheyenne* (Wyoming) *Daily Leader,* 25 July 1878.

3. John K. Rollinson, *Wyoming Cattle Trails* (Caldwell, Idaho: Caxton Printers, 1948), pp. 21-27.

4. Ibid., p. 27.

2. COWBOY CLOTHING

1. Bert Hall, *Roundup Years: Old Muddy to the Black Hills* (Kennebec, South Dakota: Last Roundup Club, 1956), p. 120.

2. Edward C. Abbott and Helena Huntington Smith, *We Pointed Them North* (New York: Farrar and Rinehart, 1939), p. 8.

3. John M. Hunter, *The Trail Drivers of Texas*, volume 2 (George W. Saunders, 1923), p. 52.

4. Abbott and Smith, *We Pointed Them North*, p. 48.

5. John K. Rollinson, *Pony Trails in Wyoming* (Caldwell, Idaho: Caxton Printers, 1941), p. 108.

6. Floyd C. Bard, *Horse Wrangler: Sixty Years in the Saddle in Wyoming and Montana* (Norman, Oklahoma: University of Oklahoma Press, 1960), p. 95.

7. Rollinson, *Wyoming Cattle Trails*, p. 119.

8. Montgomery Ward, 1874-75 *Catalog, number 12*, pp. 30-31. American Heritage Center collection, University of Wyoming, Laramie, Wyoming.

9. Montgomery Ward, 1878 *Catalog, number 20*, pp. 52-53. American Heritage Center collection.

10. "Stetson: Hat of the West," *Rodeo News*, September 1980, p. [21].

11. Douglas Branch, *The Cowboy and His Interpreters* (New York: Cooper Square Publishers, 1961), p. 21.

12. Sears, Roebuck *1900 Catalog* (reprint), (Northfield, Illinois: Digest Books, 1970), p. 556.

13. "El Sombrero: Jack W. Pilley," *Santa Barbara Historical Society Noticias 9* (Spring 1963): pp. 26-27; also, Elbert Hubbard, *Little Journeys to the Homes of Great Businessmen: John B. Stetson* (East Avroka, New York: Roycrofters, 1911), pp. 25-33.

14. Lewis Nordyke, "John B., The Hat of the West," *Quarter Horse Journal*, September 1951, p. 9.

15. E. Hough, *The Story of the Cowboy* (New York: D. Appleton and Company, 1897), p. 54.

16. Ibid.

17. John R. Barrows, *Ubet* (Caldwell, Idaho: Caxton Printers, 1936), p. 154.

18. Wallace I. Robertson, "The Stetson Story," *Nevada Magazine*, Spring 1973, pp. 27-31.

19. Jim Russell, *Bob Fudge, Texas Trail Driver: Montana-Wyoming Cowboy, 1862-1933* (Denver: Big Mountain Press, 1962), pp. 70-71.

20 Sears, Roebuck, *1900 Catalog*, p. 556.

21. Montgomery Ward, *Summer 1883 Catalog*, pp. 82-83. American Heritage Center collection.

22. Montgomery Ward, 1890 *Catalog, number 47*, pp. 277-278. American Heritage Center collection.

23. Montgomery Ward, 1910 *Catalog, number 79*, p. 852. American Heritage Center collection.

24. Mary Hagen, "Big Hats of Cheyenne," *In Wyoming*, October/November 1976, pp. 27-29.

25 Joseph Mora, *Trail Dust and Saddle Leather* (New York: Charles Scribner's Sons, 1946), p. 41.

26. Philip Ashton Rollins, *The Cowboy: An Unconventional History of Civilization on the Old-Time Cattle Range* (Albuquerque, New Mexico: University of New Mexico Press, 1936), p. 157.

27. Bard, *Horse Wrangler*, pp. 80-81.

28. Abbott and Smith, *We Pointed Them North*, pp. 20-21.

29. Bard, *Horse Wrangler*, p. 52.

30. Montgomery Ward, 1874 *Catalog, number 12*, p. 35.

31. Abbott and Smith, *We Pointed Them North*, p. 47.

32. Montgomery Ward, 1885 *Catalog, number 39*, p. 111. American Heritage Center collection.

33. Rollinson, *Pony Trails in Wyoming*, p. 40.

34. Ibid.

35. Rollins, *The Cowboy*, p. 109.

36. Don Rickey Jr., *$10 Horse and $40 Saddle* (Ft. Collins, Colorado: The Old Army Press, 1976), p. 34.

37. Abbott and Smith, *We Pointed Them North*, p. 169.

38. Bard, *Horse Wrangler*, pp. 10 and 11.

39. Rollinson, *Pony Trails in Wyoming*, p. 39.

40. Ibid.

41. Rickey, *$10 Horse and $40 Saddle*, p. 35.

42. White and Davis, 1921 *Catalog, number 17*, pp. 45-53. Joseph Palen collection, Cheyenne, Wyoming.

43. Nellie Snyder Yost, *Boss Cowman: Recollections of Ed Lemmon, 1857-1946* (Lincoln, Nebraska: University of Nebraska Press, 1969), pp. 303-304.

44. N. Porter Saddle and Harness Company, 1930 *Catalog, number 18*, p. 109. Palen collection.

45. Bard, *Horse Wrangler*, p. 20.

46. U.S. Army, *Uniforms and Equipment*, Quartermaster General of the Army, Philadelphia Depot, 1889, p. 56.

47. Rickey, *$10 Horse and $40 Saddle*, pp. 26-27.

48. Jean Brainerd, "Adventures of an Englishman in Cummins City: Letters from Robert Mills," *Annals of Wyoming*, 60 (Fall 1988):33.

49. Keith Eubank and Thyllis Tortora, *A Survey of Historic Costume* (New York: Fairchild Publications, 1989), p. 285.

50. Sears, Roebuck, *1902 Catalog*; reprint edition, New York: Dover Publications, 1969), pp. 975-76.

51. Montgomery Ward, 1909 *Catalog, number 78*, pp. 503-504. American Heritage Center collection.

52. Yost, *Boss Cowman*, p. 221.

53. Rickey, *$10 Horse and $40 Saddle*, p. 38.

54. Rollinson, *Pony Trails in Wyoming*, pp. 33-34.

55. Hough, *The Story of the Cowboy*, p. 52.

56. Alison Gernsheim, *Victorian and Edwardian Fashion: A Photographic Survey* (New York: Dover Publications, 1981), pp. 36-40.

57. Rickey, *$10 Horse and $40 Saddle*, p. 24.

58. Ibid., p. 40.

59. Abbott and Smith, *We Pointed Them North*, p. 205.

60. Rickey, *$10 Horse and $40 Saddle*, p. 40.

61. Hough, *The Story of the Cowboy*, p. 57.

62. Montgomery Ward, 1886 *Catalog, number 40*, p. 221. American Heritage Center collection.

63. Bard, *Horse Wrangler*, p. 26.

64. Edgar B. Bronson, *Cowboy Life on the Western Plains: The Reminiscenses of a Ranchman* (New York: Grosset and Dunlap, 1910), p. 117.

65. Montgomery Ward, 1874-75 *Catalog, number 12*, p. 39.

66. Rickey, *$10 Horse and $40 Saddle*, p. 44.

67. Hough, *The Story of the Cowboy*, p. 53.

68. Rollinson, *Pony Trails in Wyoming*, p. 126.

69. Ibid., p. 301.

70. Abbott and Smith, *We Pointed Them North*, p. 205.

71. Ibid., p. 7.

72. *Patent Office Gazette*, July 1882, Volume #22, p. 1727. Patent Serial Number 66968.

73. Rollinson, *Pony Trails in Wyoming*, p. 149.

74. Montgomery Ward, 1885 *Catalog, number 39* p. 100; 1886 *Catalog, number 40*, p. 224.

75. Letter to Connie Lindmier from the Office of the Secretary of State of Wyoming, July 1988. Corporation Information Records, DCM-001.

76. Bard, *Horse Wrangler*, p. 82.

77. Rollinson, *Wyoming Cattle Trails*, p. 133.

78. Ramon F. Adams, *The Old-Time Cowhand* (New York: Macmillan, 1961), p. 98.

79. Rollinson, *Wyoming Cattle Trails*, pp. 66 and 67.

80. Hunter, *The Trail Drivers of Texas*, p. 381.

81. Rollinson, *Pony Trails in Wyoming*, p. 173.

82. Hough, *The Story of the Cowboy*, p. 56.

83. Rollinson, *Pony Trails in Wyoming*, p. 108.

84. Judy Crandall, *Cowgirls: Early Images and Collectibles* (Atglen, PA: Schiffer Publishing Ltd, 1994).

3. RIDING GEAR

1. John A. Kopec, "Cowboy Chaps," *Old West Magazine,* 1979, p. 77.

2. Abbott and Smith, *We Pointed Them North*, p. 8.

3. Rollinson, *Pony Trails in Wyoming*, p. 287.

4. Harry Williams, "Cowboy Life," WPA Project Files 201, p. 1. Historical Research, Wyoming State Museum, Cheyenne, Wyoming.

5. R. T. Frazier, 1907 *Catalog, number 8*, p. 70. Palen collection.

6. Rollinson, *Pony Trails in Wyoming*, p. 299.

7. Hamley and Company, 1913 *Catalog, number 3*, p. 92. Palen collection.

8. Barrows, *Ubet*, p. 153.

9. Yost, *Boss Cowman*, p. 302.

10. Hough, *The Story of the Cowboy*, pp. 62 and 63.

11. Bud Cowan, *Range Rider* (Garden City, New York: Sun Dial Press, 1930), p. 226.

12. Rollinson, *Pony Trails in Wyoming*, p. 321.

13. Don Hedgpeth, "Una Buena Reata (The Good Rope)," *Horse Lovers Magazine*, March/April 1968, p. 65.

14. David Dary, *Cowboy Culture: A Saga of Five Centuries* (New York: Alfred A. Knopf, 1981), p. 155.

15. Bob Robertson, "Reatas, Cabretos & Mecates," *Cattleman Magazine*, June 1965, p. [look up].

16. Rollinson, *Pony Trails in Wyoming*, p. 300.

17. Barrows, *Ubet*, pp. 123-125.

18. Jane Pattie, "The Western Rope," *Texas and Southwestern Horseman*, December 1964, pp. 24-25.

19. Stockman and Farmer, *1929 catalog*, p. 44. Palen collection.

20. Yost, *Boss Cowman*, p. 195.

21. Rollinson, *Pony Trails in Wyoming*, p. 287.

22. Bronson, *Cowboy Life on the Western Plains*, p. 24.

23. Barrows, *Ubet*, pp. 162-163.

24. Rollinson, *Pony Trails in Wyoming*, p. 199.

25. Bard, *Horse Wrangler*, p. 130.

26. Abbott and Smith, *We Pointed Them North*, pp. 28-29.

27. Yost, *Boss Cowman*, p. 302.

28. Winchester Firearms Company, 1899 *Catalog, number 63*; reprint edition, Prescott, Arizona: Wolfe Publishing, 1990, p. 6.

29. Harold McCracken, *The American Cowboy* (Garden City, New York: Doubleday, 1973), p. 146.

30. Barrows, *Ubet*, pp. 162-163.

31. Cowan, *Range Rider*, p. 28.

32. Bronson, *Cowboy Life on the Western Plains*, p. 58.

33. Ibid., pp. 90-91.

34. Ibid., p. 98.

35. Barrows, *Ubet*, p. 174.

36. Rollinson, *Wyoming Cattle Trails*, p. 270.

37. Ibid., p. 57.

38. Ibid., p. 57.

39. Williams, *"Cowboy Life,"* p. 2.

40. *Hough*, p. 59.

41. Abbott and Smith, *We Pointed Them North*, p. 246.

42. Bronson, *Cowboy Life on the Western Plains*, p. 25.

43. Barrows, *Ubet*, pp. 155-156.

44. Rickey, *$10 Horse and $40 Saddle*, p. 76.

45. Bard, *Horse Wrangler*, p. 25.

46. Abbott and Smith, *We Pointed Them North*, p. 95.

47. Ibid., p. 32.

48. Cynthia Rhoades, "Knives of the Cowboy," *The Blade Magazine*, March/April 1987, p. 33.

4. Horse Gear

1. Rollinson, *Wyoming Cattle Trails*, pp. 36-37.

2. Russel H. Beatie, *Saddles* (Norman, Oklahoma: University of Oklahoma Press, 1981), pp. 50-57.

3. Ibid., p. 128.

4. Ibid., pp. 50-57.

5. Ibid., pp. 76-77.

6. Ibid., pp. 67-71.

7. Ibid., p. 129.

8. Ibid., pp. 71-76.

9. Montgomery Ward, *1883 Catalog*, pp. 102-103.

10. Bard, *Horse Wrangler*, p. 204.

11. Hall, *Roundup Years*, p. 120.

12. E. Hough, *The Story of the Cowboy*, pp. 64-65.

13. Rollinson, *Pony Trails in Wyoming*, p. 35.

14. D. E. Walker, Visalia Saddle Company, *1900 Catalog*; reprint edition (Millwood, New York: Zon International Publishing, 1991), p. 8.

15. R. T. Frazier, *1907 Catalog*, p.14.

16. Rollinson, *Pony Trails in Wyoming*, p. 173.

17. Beatie, *Saddles*, p. 57.

18. Denver Manufacturing Company, *1883 Catalog*, p. 165. Palen collection, Cheyenne, Wyoming.

19. Charles P. Shippley, Saddlery and Mercantile Company, *Catalog*, p. 64.

20. Beatie, *Saddles*, p. 53.

21. Adams, *The Old-Time Cowhand*, p. 112.

22. Sammy Sisco, "Types & Kinds of Stirrups," *Western Horseman*, November/December 1974, p. 29.

23. Steve Nevil, Oral interview, 3 February 1992. Thomas Lindmier collection, South Pass City, Wyoming.

24. J. S. Collins & Company, *1886 Catalog*, p. 56.

25. R. T. Frazier, *1907 Catalog*, p. 77.

26. Rollinson, *Pony Trails in Wyoming*, p. 123.

27. R. T. Frazier, *1907 Catalog*, p. 9.

28. Ibid., p. 5.

29. Beatie, *Saddles*, pp. 110-111.

30. Rollinson, *Wyoming Cattle Trails*, p. 37.

31. Mora, *Trail Dust and Saddle Leather*, p. 108.

32. R. T. Frazier, *1907 Catalog*, pp. 82-83.

33. Reuben B. Mullins, *Pulling Leather* (Glendo, Wyoming: High Plains Press, 1988), p. 89.

34. D. E. Walker, Visilia Stock Saddle Company, *1900 Catalog*, p. 41.

35. R. T. Frazier, *1907 catalog*, p. 82.

36. Joseph Palen, Oral interview, 16 March 1992, Cheyenne, Wyoming. Thomas Lindmier collection, South Pass City, Wyoming.

37. White and Davis Company, *1921 Catalog*, pp. 127-128.

38. A cricket is a roller device placed in the mouthpiece. *See* Glossary.

39. D. E. Walker, Visalia Stock Saddle Company, *1900 Catalog*, pp. 38-39.

40. Bard, *Horse Wrangler*, p. 127.

41. Correspondence, Frank Meanea to Holdon Peterson, no date. Holdon Peterson collection, Historical Research, Wyoming State Museum, Cheyenne, Wyoming.

42. Correspondence, Holdon Peterson to John B. Kendrick, 12 July 1889. Holden Peterson collection, Historical Research, Wyoming State Museum, Cheyenne, Wyoming.

43. R. T. Frazier, *1907 catalog*, p. 73.

44. Barrows, *Ubet*, p. 166.

45. Rollinson, *Pony Trails in Wyoming*, pp. 286-287.

46. Palen interview, 17 March 1992.

47. Adams, *The Old-Time Cowhand*, p. 119.

5. BEDROLLS, CAMP EQUIPMENT AND CHUCK WAGONS

1. Rollinson, *Pony Trails in Wyoming*, p. 108.

2. Correspondence, John B. Kendrick to G. E. Lemmon, Lemmon, South Dakota, 26 November 1927. Kendrick collection, American Heritage Center, University of Wyoming, Laramie, Wyoming.

3. Abbott and Smith, *We Pointed Them North*, p. 8.

4. Russell, *Bob Fudge, Texas Trail Driver*, p. 22.

5. Williams, "Cowboy Life," p. 3.

6. Richey, *$10 Horse and $40 Saddle*, p. 102.

7. Ibid., p. 102.

8. Williams, *Cowboy Life*, p. 9.

9. Yost, *Boss Cowman*, p. 13.

10. Adams, *The Old-Time Cowhand*, p. 100.

11. Rickey, *$10 Horse and $40 Saddle*, pp. 107-108.

12. Rollinson, *Pony Trails in Wyoming*, p. 39.

13. Bard, *Horse Wrangler*, p. 18.

14. Rollins, *The Cowboy*, p. 155.

15. Bard, *Horse Wrangler*, p. 186.

16. Rollins, *The Cowboy*, p. 129

17. Berkebile, *Horse-Drawn Commercial Vehicles* (New York: Dover Publications, 1989), p. 36.

18. Rollinson, *Pony Trails in Wyoming*, pp. 40-41.

19. Barrows, *Ubet*, p. 173-174.

GLOSSARY

(Saddle terms are illustrated on page 115)

Armas—Large leather flaps permanently attached to the saddle and thrown back over the legs to protect the vaquero. Predecessor of the cowboy's chaps.

Armitas—Meaning little armor, a variety of short chaps, more commonly known as chinks.

Bucking rolls—Padded leather attachments for the slick fork saddle which aided the cowboy while riding a bucking horse. When the swell fork saddle was later developed, it eliminated the need for bucking rolls.

Center-Fire Saddle—A saddle with only one cinch which is rigged in the center.

Chaparreras or Chaps—Leather pants to be worn over trousers as protection against brush or cold weather.

Chinks—Short chaps extending to just below the knee.

Concho/Concha—The words are synonymous for an ornamental disk which commonly adorned saddles, spur straps and chaps.

Corona—A heavy carpet saddle pad with leather edge binding and reinforcements.

Cricket—A roller device placed on a bit's mouthpiece which provides something the horse can play with while the bit is in its mouth. A horse will work this cricket with his tongue, using it as a pacifier.

Dally Roping—Taking two or more turns around the saddle horn with the home end of the rope, after having roped an animal, from the Spanish *dur la vuelta*.

Hackamore—Usually an ordinary halter carrying reins instead of a lead rope. The horse is controlled by presenting pressure on the nose. The term was corrupted from the Spanish word *jaquima*.

Hard and Fast Roping—When the rope is permanently tied to the saddle horn before being used for roping.

Honda—A fixed eye or small loop attached to one end of a lariat. The main line of the lariat is then fed through this eye and creates a loop for roping livestock. It usually has a leather or rawhide "burner" which protects the rope from the friction created when the lariat passes through the honda.

Jaranos—A border Mexican word for a stiff-brimmed fine fur hat.

Jaranos Pallano—A hat style introduced by the J.B. Stetson Company.

Jaranos Poblanos—A stiff-brimmed fine fur hat imported from Puebla, Mexico.

Latigo—A leather strap used to attach a cinch to a saddle.

Maguey Rope—Rope made from the fibers of the maguey plant.

Mecate or MacCarty—A horse hair rope about 20 feet long.

Mochila—A leather saddle cover for early stock saddles. The Pony Express riders utilized a removable mochila with pockets for carrying mail.

Noseband or Bosal—A leather strap or braided leather part used in conjunction with a hackamore which forms a band over or just above a horse's nostrils.

Nutria—The commercial name for the soft brown fur of the coypu, sometimes dyed to give the appearance of beaver.

Panniers—Large bags for carrying cargo on the pack saddle.

Port—The curved portion of the bar, or mouth-piece, of a curb bit.

Reata—Term from the Spanish *la reata* meaning to re-tie. A rawhide rope.

Rim-Fire or Double Rigged Saddle—A saddle with two cinches.

Romal—From the Spanish *el ramal* meaning branch road. It is a quirt-like affair attached to the saddle end of closed reins which is used much like a quirt.

Rowels—The wheels of a spur.

Shank—The cheek-piece or side-bar of a bit. The shank is also the portion of the spur to which the rowel is attached.

Slicker—A yellow or black rain coat.

Soogan or Sugan—A heavy comforter or quilt that forms part of cowboy's bed roll.

Tackaberry—A hooked-type device which attaches to the latigo. The hook portion is then secured to the ring of the cinch, allowing a fast and easy means of cinching the saddle. Not commonly employed because it had to be adjusted for each individual horse.

Tapaderos—Leather covers on stirrups used to protect the rider's feet and the stirrups.

Vacquero—The term used in southwestern America for a person who herds cattle, the Mexican cowboy.

Warbag—A seamless sack the cowboy used to carry extra clothing and personal items.

BIBLIOGRAPHY

Books:

Abbott, Edward C., and Smith, Helena Huntington. *We Pointed Them North: Recollections of a Cowpuncher*. New York: Farrar and Rinehart, 1939.

Adams, Ramon Frederick. *The Old-Time Cowhand*. New York: Macmillan, 1961.

Ahlborn, Richard E. *Man Made Mobile: Early Saddles of Western North America*. Washington, D.C.: Smithsonian Institution Press, 1980.

Bard, Floyd C. *Horse Wrangler: Sixty Years in the Saddle in Wyoming and Montana*. Norman, Oklahoma: University of Oklahoma Press, 1960.

Barrows, John R. *Ubet*. Caldwell, Idaho: Caxton Printers, 1936.

Beatie, Russel H. *Saddles*. Norman, Oklahoma: University of Oklahoma Press, 1981.

Berkebile, Don H. *Horse-Drawn Commercial Vehicles*. New York: Dover Publications, 1989.

Branch, Douglas. *The Cowboy and His Interpreters*. New York: Cooper Square Publishers, 1961.

Bronson, Edgar Beecher. *Cowboy Life on the Western Plains: The Reminiscences of a Ranchman*. New York: Grosset and Dunlap, 1910.

Bryk, Nancy Villa. *American Dress Pattern Catalogs, 1873-1909*. New York: Dover Publications, 1988.

Clay, John. *My Life on the Range*. Norman, Oklahoma: University of Oklahoma Press, 1962.

Coolidge, Dane. *Old California Cowboys*. New York: E. P. Dutton, 1939.

Cowan, Bud. *Range Rider*. Garden City, New York: Sun Dial Press, 1930).

Dale, Edward Everett. *Cow Country*. Second reprint, Norman, Oklahoma: University of Oklahoma Press, 1968.

Dana, Richard Henry. *Two Years Before the Mast*. New York: World Publishing, 1946.

Dary, David. *Cowboy Culture: A Saga of Five Centuries*. New York: Alfred A. Knopf, 1981.

Doubleday, Russell. *Cattle-Ranch to College*. New York: Doubleday and McClure, 1899.

Eubank, Keith, and Tortora, Thyllis. *A Survey of Historic Costume*. New York: Fairchild Publications, 1989.

Gernsheim, Alison. *Victorian and Edwardian Fashion: A Photographic Survey*. New York: Dover Publications, 1981.

Goff, Richard, and McCaffree, Robert H. *Century in the Saddle, 1867-1967*. Denver: Colorado Women's Centennial Commission, 1967.

Gorsline, Douglas. *What People Wore*. New York: Bonanza Books, 1952.

Hall, Bert. *Roundup Years: Old Muddy to Black Hills*. Second printing, Kennebec, South Dakota: Last Roundup Club, 1956.

Hendrix, John. *If I Can Do It Horseback*. Austin, Texas: University of Texas Press, 1964.

Hough, E. *The Story of the Cowboy*. New York: D. Appleton and Company, 1897.

Hubbard, Elbert. *Little Journeys to the Homes of Great Business Men: John B. Stetson*. East Avroka, New York: Roycrofters, 1911.

Hunter, John Marvin. *The Trail Drivers of Texas*; volume II. George W. Saunders and the Old Time Trail Drivers' Association, 1923.

James, W. S. *Cow-boy Life in Texas or 27 Years a Maverick.* Chicago: M. A. Donohue, 1893.

Kennedy, Michael S. *Cowboys and Cattlemen.* New York: Hastings House, 1964.

McCracken, Harold. *The American Cowboy.* Garden City, New York: Doubleday, 1973.

McDowell, Bart. *The American Cowboy: In Life and Legend.* New York: National Geographic Society, 1972.

Marriott, Alice. *Hell on Horses and Women.* Norman, Oklahoma: University of Oklahoma Press, 1953.

Mora, Joseph. *Trail Dust and Saddle Leather.* New York: Charles Scribner's Sons, 1946.

Mullins, Reuben B. *Pulling Leather.* Glendo, Wyoming: High Plains Press, 1988.

Post, C. C. *Ten Years a Cowboy.* Chicago: Rhodes and McClure, 1897.

Rickey, Don. *$10 Horse and $40 Saddle.* Fort Collins, Colorado: Old Army Press, 1976.

Rollins, Philip Ashton. *The Cowboy: An Unconventional History of Civilization on the Old-Time Cattle Range.* Albuquerque, New Mexico: University of New Mexico Press, 1936.

Rollinson, John K. *Pony Trails in Wyoming.* Caldwell, Idaho: Caxton Printers, 1941.

_____. *Wyoming Cattle Trails.* Caldwell, Idaho: Caxton Printers, 1948.

Russell, Jim. *Bob Fudge, Texas Trail Driver: Montana-Wyoming Cowboy, 1862-1933.* Denver: Big Mountain Press, 1962.

Spring, Agnes Wright. *Seventy Years: History of the Wyoming Stock Growers Association.* Cheyenne: Wyoming Stock Growers Association, Cheyenne, 1942.

U.S. Army. *Uniforms and Equipment.* Quartermaster General of the Army, Philadelphia Depot, 1889.

Vernam, Glenn R. *Man on Horseback.* New York: Harper and Row, 1964.

Waddil, O. B. *Saddle Strings.* Gordon, Nebraska: Tri-State Old Time Cowboys Association, 1976.

Yost, Nellie Snyder. *Boss Cowman: The Recollections of Ed Lemmon, 1857-1946.* Lincoln, Nebraska: University of Nebraska Press, 1969.

_____. *The Call of the Range.* Denver: Sage Books, 1966.

CATALOGS

Arizona Saddlery Company. Catalog No. 5, 1905. Gillette, Wyoming and Prescott, Arizona. Joseph Palen collection, Cheyenne, Wyoming.

Blucher, G. C. Boot Maker Catalog, 1915. Cheyenne, Wyoming. Joseph Palen collection, Cheyenne, Wyoming.

Collins, J. S. & Company. Catalog, 1886. Joseph Palen collection, Cheyenne, Wyoming.

Denver Manufacturing Company. Catalog, 1883. Joseph Palen collection, Cheyenne, Wyoming.

Ernst, Otto F. Cowboy Equipment Catalog No. 14, 1931. Sheridan, Wyoming. Joseph Palen collection, Cheyenne, Wyoming.

Frazier, R. T. Saddle Catalog No. 8, 1907. Pueblo, Colorado. Joseph Palen collection, Cheyenne, Wyoming.

Hamley and Company. Catalog No. 3, 1913. Pendleton, Oregon. Joseph Palen collection, Cheyenne, Wyoming.

Hyer, C. H. and Sons. Catalog No. 12, 1917. Olathe, Kansas. Joseph Palen collection, Cheyenne, Wyoming.

Meyer, Max J. Stetson Hat Catalog, late 1920's. Cheyenne, Wyoming. Joseph Palen collection, Cheyenne, Wyoming.

Miller, Blake. Famous Hand Made Saddles Catalog No. 11, 1921. Cheyenne, Wyoming. Joseph Palen collection, Cheyenne, Wyoming.

Montgomery Ward and Company. Catalog No. 12, 1874-75. American Heritage Center, University of Wyoming, Laramie, Wyoming.

_____. Catalog No. 20, 1878. American Heritage Center, University of Wyoming, Laramie, Wyoming.

_____. Catalog, 1883. American Heritage Center, University of Wyoming, Laramie, Wyoming.

_____. Catalog No. 39, 1885. American Heritage Center, University of Wyoming, Laramie, Wyoming.

_____. Catalog No. 40, 1886. American Heritage Center, University of Wyoming, Laramie, Wyoming.

_____. Catalog No. 47, 1890. American Heritage Center, University of Wyoming, Laramie, Wyoming.

_____. Catalog No. 78, 1909. American Heritage Center, University of Wyoming, Laramie, Wyoming.

_____. Catalog No. 79, 1910. American Heritage Center, University of Wyoming, Laramie, Wyoming.

Olzer, Frank Catalog, 1905. Gillette, Wyoming. Joseph Palen collection, Cheyenne, Wyoming.

Porter, N. Saddle and Harness Company Catalog No. 18, 1930. Phoenix, Arizona. Joseph Palen collection, Cheyenne, Wyoming.

Prior, George W. Hat Company Catalog, Spring and Summer 1905. Denver, Colorado. Joseph Palen collection, Cheyenne, Wyoming.

Remington, E., and Sons. Catalog, 1877. Reprint edition, Union City, Tennessee: Pioneer Press, n.d..

Schoellkopf Company. Saddlery Catalog, 1895. Wallace Irving Robertson collection, American Heritage Center, University of Wyoming, Laramie, Wyoming.

Sears, Roebuck and Company. Catalog, 1900. Reprint edition, Northfield, Illinois: Digest Books, 1970.

_____. Catalog, 1902. Reprint edition, New York: Bounty Books, 1969.

Shippley, Charles P. Saddlery and Mercantile Company Catalog. Catalog No. 12, 1913. Kansas City, Missouri. Joseph Palen collection, Cheyenne, Wyoming.

Stockman and Farmer Supply Company. Fall and Winter Catalog No. 29, 1926-1927. Denver, Colorado. Joseph Palen collection, Cheyenne, Wyoming.

_____. Spring Catalog No. 34, 1929. Denver, Colorado. Joseph Palen collection, Cheyenne, Wyoming.

Walker, D. E. Visalia Stock Saddle Company Catalog, 1900. Reprint edition, Millwood, New York: Zon International Publishing, 1991.

White and Davis. Summer and Spring Catalog No. 17, 1921. Pueblo, Colorado. Joseph Palen collection, Cheyenne, Wyoming.

Winchester Firearms. Catalog No. 63, 1899. Reprint edition, Prescott, Arizona: Wolfe Publishing, 1990.

Magazines, Newspapers, Unpublished Documents

Brainerd, Jean, editor. "Adventures of an Englishman in Cummins City: Letters from Robert Mills." *Annals of Wyoming*, Volume 60, No. 2, Fall, 1988.

Cheyenne (Wyoming) Daily Leader, 25 July 1878.

_____, 10 November 1881.

"El Sombrero: Jack W. Pilley." *Santa Barbara Historical Society Noticias*, Spring 1963.

Hagen, Mary. "Big Hats of Cheyenne." *In Wyoming*, October/November 1976.

Hedgpeth, Don. "Una Buena Reata (The Good Rope)." *Horse Lovers Magazine*, March/April 1968.

Hewitt, Bob. "Chaps for the Cowboy." *Western Horseman*, November 1983

"The Hobble: A Cowboy's Riding Insurance." *Tack Room Journal*, May 1978.

Kendrick, John B. Correspondence with G. E. Lemmon, 26 November 1927, Lemmon, South Dakota. Kendrick collection, American Heritage Center, University of Wyoming, Laramie, Wyoming.

Kopec, John A. "Cowboy Chaps." *Old West*, 1979.

Meanea, Frank. Correspondence to Holdon Peterson, undated. Peterson collection, Historical Research, Wyoming State Museum, Cheyenne, Wyoming.

"Mormon Hobbles." *Tack Room Journal*, January 1979.

Nevil, Steve. Oral interview, 3 February 1992. Thomas Lindmier collection, South Pass City, Wyoming.

Nordyke, Lewis. "John B.: The Hat of the West." *Quarter Horse Journal*, September 1951.

Palen, Joseph. Oral interview, 16 March 1992. Thomas Lindmier collection, South Pass City, Wyoming.

Patent Office Gazette, July 1882.

Pattie, Jane. "The Western Rope." *Texas and Southwestern Horseman*, December 1964.

Peterson, Holdon. Correspondence to John B. Kendrick, 12 July 1889. Peterson collection, Historical Research, Wyoming State Museum, Cheyenne, Wyoming.

Rhoades, Cynthia Vannoy. "Knives of the Cowboy." *The Blade Magazine*, March/April, 1987.

Robertson, Bob. "Reatas, Cabretos and Mecates." *Cattleman Magazine*, June 1965.

Robertson, Wallace I. "The Stetson Story." *Nevada Magazine*, Spring 1973.

Schipman, Henry, Jr. "Catch Rope South of the Border." *Western Horseman*, September 1969.

Sisco, Sammy. "Types and Kinds of Stirrups." *Western Horseman*, November/December 1974.

"Stetson: Hat of the West." *Rodeo News*, September 1980.

"Through the Years: James Hardman Family." Unpublished manuscript (No. 5761), American Heritage Center, University of Wyoming, Laramie, Wyoming.

Walters, Keith. "Chinks and Woolies." *Western Horseman*, May 1986.

_____. "Cowboy Wrist Cuffs." *Western Horseman*, November 1986.

Williams, Harry. "Cowboy Life." WPA Writer's Project Files, Historical Research, Wyoming State Museum, Cheyenne, Wyoming.

← Authors Tom Lindmier
and Steve Mount enjoy col-
lecting historic cowboy gear
and occasionally try it on
for size.

Steven R. Mount was born in Afton, Wyoming. His family came west as part of a Mormon handcart company in
1851. He is a sixth generation Wyoming-ite whose distant
grandfather homesteaded in the Star Valley, Wyoming
area. While never having the opportunity to operate his
family's ranch in Star Valley, Steve has nevertheless carried
on the ranching and stockraising tradition by working
part time for ranchers. Steve's great grandmother was the
first licensed woman outfitter in the state of Wyoming
and provided this service until the mid 1950s.

Steve attended college in Idaho after leaving the Army
in 1977. He has researched the spectrum of western history throughout his years and is now a knowledgeable his-
torian in his own right. His major interests are in the
fields of the cowboy, stage transportation, frontier military history and settlement of the west. Steve is currently
employed by the FMC Corporation and is a captain in
the Wyoming Army National Guard.

Thomas A. Lindmier was raised in Douglas, Wyoming.
He holds a Bachelor's degree in history from the
University of Wyoming. Upon completing college, Tom
began a career in historic site development, interpretation
and management. Currently he is the Superintendent of
South Pass City State Historic Site. Tom is a generalist in
western history with a strong interest in the western
ranching history, military history, transportation history
and general western expansion.

Tom's great uncle and grandfather both owned and
operated large ranches north of Douglas where he spent
his summers during his early youth. His uncle and cousins
now manage these holdings.

Tom and Steve have given presentations on the
Northern Plains cowboy at the Gene Autry Western
Heritage Museum, Wyoming Centennial celebrations at
the Big Horn Canyon National Recreation Area, and at
the Wyoming Territorial Park in Laramie, Wyoming.

This book was printed
on acid-free, recycled paper.
The text is set in eleven point Adobe Garamond.
Display and extract is in Lutahline
by Judith Sutcliffe,
the Electronic Typographer.